Core concepts in therapy

Series editor: Michael Jacobs

Over the last ten years a significant shift has taken place in the relations between representatives of different schools of therapy. Instead of the competitive and often hostile reactions we once expected from each other, therapists from different points of the spectrum of approaches are much more interested in where they overlap and where they differ. There is a new sense of openness to cross orientation learning.

The series *In Search of a Therapist* also published by the Open University Press has already contributed in a major way to this process of rapprochement and dialogue, examining the way in which therapists differ or overlap in the way they work with a particular client or presenting set of issues. The next step is to examine theoretical models, and the commonalities and difference in the use of technical concepts, which form the language of psychotherapy.

The *Core Concepts in Therapy* series compares and contrasts the use of similar terms across a range of the therapeutic models, and seeks to identify where different terms appear to denote similar concepts. Each book is authored by two therapists, each one from a distinctly different orientation; and where possible each one from a different continent, so that an international dimension becomes a feature of this network of ideas.

Each of these short volumes examines a key concept in psychological therapy, setting out comparative positions in a spirit of free and critical enquiry, but without the need to prove one model superior to another. The books are fully referenced and point beyond themselves to the wider literature on each topic.

Forthcoming and published titles:
Dinesh Bhugra and Dilys Davies: *Models of Psychopathology*
Paul Brinich and Christopher Shelly: *The Self and Personality Structure*
Dawn Freshwater and Chris Robertson: *Emotions and Needs*
Jan Grant and Jim Crawley: *Transference and Projection*
Richard J. Hazler and Nick Barwick: *The Therapeutic Environment*
John Rowan and Michael Jacobs: *The Therapist's Use of Self*
Lynn Sieser and Colin Wastell: *Interventions and Techniques*
Val Simanowitz and Peter Pearce: *Personality Development*
Gabrielle Syme and Jenifer Elton Wilson: *Objectives and Outcomes*
Nick Totton and Michael Jacobs: *Character and Personality Types*
Kenneth C. Wallis and James L. Poulton: *Internalization*

THE THERAPEUTIC ENVIRONMENT

Core conditions for facilitating therapy

Richard J. Hazler
and
Nick Barwick

Open University Press
Buckingham • Philadelphia

Open University Press
Celtic Court
22 Ballmoor
Buckingham
MK18 1XW

email: enquiries@openup.co.uk
world wide web: www.openup.co.uk
and
325 Chestnut Street
Philadelphia, PA 19106, USA

First Published 2001

1003070260

A catalogue record of this book is available from the British Library

ISBN   0 335 20282 9 (pb)   0 335 20283 7 (hb)

Library of Congress Cataloging-in-Publication Data
The therapeutic environment: core conditions for facilitating
therapy / Richard J. Hazler and Nick Barwick.
    p. cm. – (Core concepts in therapy)
    Includes bibliographical references and index.
    ISBN 0–335–20283–7 – ISBN 0–335–20282–9 (pbk.)
    1. Psychodynamic psychotherapy. I. Hazler, Richard J.
II. Barwick, Nick, 1959– III. Series.
RC489.P72 T48 2001
616.89'14–dc21   00–060638

Typeset by Graphicraft Limited, Hong Kong
Printed in Great Britain by The Cromwell Press, Trowbridge

Contents

Series editor's preface

A major aspect of intellectual and cultural life in the twentieth century has been the study of psychology – present of course for many centuries in practical form and expression in the wisdom and insight to be found in spirituality, in literature and in the dramatic arts, as well as in arts of healing and guidance, both in the East and West. In parallel with the deepening interest in the inner processes of character and relationships in the novel and theatre in the nineteenth century, psychiatry reformulated its understanding of the human mind, and encouraged, in those brave enough to challenge the myths of mental illness, new methods of exploration of psychological processes.

The second half of the twentieth century in particular witnessed an explosion of interest both in theories about personality, psychological development, cognition and behaviour, as well as in the practice of therapy, or perhaps more accurately, the therapies. It also saw, as is not uncommon in any intellectual discipline, battles between theories and therapists of different persuasions, particularly between psychoanalysis and behavioural psychology, and each in turn with humanistic and transpersonal therapies, as well as within the major schools themselves. Such arguments are not surprising, and indeed objectively can be seen as healthy – potentially promoting greater precision in research, alternative approaches to apparently intractable problems, and deeper understanding of the wellsprings of human thought, emotion and behaviour. It is nonetheless disturbing that for many decades there was such a degree of sniping and entrenchment of positions from therapists who should have been able to look more closely at their own responses and rivalries. It is as if diplomats had ignored their skills and knowledge and resorted in their dealings with each other to gun slinging.

The psychotherapeutic enterprise has also been an international one. There were a large number of centres of innovation, even at the beginning – Paris, Moscow, Vienna, Berlin, Zurich, London, Boston USA – and soon Edinburgh, Rome, New York, Chicago and California saw the development of different theories and therapeutic practice. Geographical location has added to the richness of the discipline, particularly identifying cultural and social differences, and widening the psychological debate to include, at least in some instances, sociological and political dimensions.

The question has to be asked – given the separate developments due to location, research interests, personal differences, and splits between the within traditions – whether what has sometimes been called 'psycho-babble' is indeed a welter of different languages describing the same phenomena through the particular jargon and theorizing of the various psychotherapeutic schools. Or are there genuine differences, which may lead sometimes to the conclusion that one school has got it right, while another has therefore got it wrong; or that there are 'horses for courses'; or, according to the Dodo principle, that 'all shall have prizes'?

The latter part of the twentieth century saw some rapprochement between the different approaches to the theory and practice of psychotherapy (and counselling), often due to the external pressures towards organizing the profession responsibly and to the high standards demanded of it by health care by the public and by the state. It is out of this budding rapprochement that there came the motivation for this series, in which a number of key concepts that lie at the heart of the psychotherapies can be compared and contrasted across the board. Some of the terms used in different traditions may prove to represent identical concepts; others may look similar, but in fact highlight quite different emphases, which may or may not prove useful to those who practise from a different perspective; other terms, apparently identical, may prove to mean something completely different in two or more schools of psychotherapy.

In order to carry out this project it seemed essential that as many of the psychotherapeutic traditions as possible should be represented in the authorship of the series; and to promote both this, and the spirit of dialogue between traditions, it seemed also desirable that there should be two authors for each book each one representing, where practicable, different orientations. It was important that the series should be truly international in its approach and therefore in its authorship; and that miracle of late twentieth-century technology, the Internet, proved to be a productive means of finding authors, as well as a remarkably efficient method of communicating, in the cases of some pairs of authors, halfway across the world.

This series therefore represents, in a new millennium, an extremely exciting development, one which as series editor I have found more and more enthralling as I have eavesdropped on the drafts shuttling back and forth between authors. Here, for the first time, the reader will find all the major concepts of all the principal schools of psychotherapy and counselling (and not a few minor ones) drawn together so that they may be compared, contrasted, and (it is my hope) above all used – used for the ongoing debate between orientations, but more importantly still, used for the benefit of clients and patients who are not at all interested in partisan positions, but in what works, or in what throws light upon their search for healing and understanding.

Michael Jacobs

Acknowledgements

My special appreciation goes to Tuncay Ergene who was such a great help in organizing an overwhelming amount of information and to JoLynn Carney whose advice, support and willingness to push was always there during the hardest times when I may have deserved the help least.

Richard Hazler

My thanks to Janet Smith of the Radcliffe Science Library for the seemingly endless supply of articles and to Douglas Betts, Anna Brave-Smith and Ian Parker for kindly checking the accuracy of my comments on theoretical orientations less familiar to me. My special thanks to Yuki Williamson, whose wise counsel has always proved so invaluable and to Carol Smart, whose patience and impatience, loving support and critical eye has played such an important part in providing me with a facilitative writing environment.

Nick Barwick

We would both like to offer our special thanks to Senior Editor, Michael Jacobs, who provided so much more than editing. For his faith, encouragement and willingness to get involved in the messy parts of such a project, we are especially grateful.

A personal introduction: core conditions of the facilitative writing environment

RICHARD HAZLER and NICK BARWICK

We (Richard Hazler and Nick Barwick) were raised continents apart (USA and England), trained differently, have diverse lives, approach issues in individualized ways and see therapy from separate perspectives (broadly Humanistic and Psychodynamic, respectively). In many ways, we are representative of the diversity of therapeutic models – and the cultures that spawned and nurtured them – that are current in the therapeutic world today. This diversity was designed to be an integral part of the book and it has certainly influenced the process and outcome of writing, just as much as it has influenced the process and outcome of our respective therapeutic practices. Consequently, in the chapters that follow, you will note differences between our written approaches just as you would were you to witness our clinical approaches in therapy sessions. This is why we want to begin with a brief description of our experience of working and writing together. In this way, we aim to place the book, and the concepts we discuss, in an immediate and personalized context.

We have different learning styles, different experiences, don't see eye-to-eye on many issues, don't think alike and don't write in the same way. At times, frustrations with each other and ourselves have taken centre stage more than the content, which we also regularly disagreed on. In fact, it would have been much easier, although we think not better, for either one of us to have written this book alone.

The differences between us caused significant problems. Yet other essential things held us together as we 'worked through' our relationship, therapy concepts and this book. In the end, the differences, doubts, anxieties and struggles were not enough to outweigh our commonalties, hopes, our alliance, our respect and our motivation to succeed and learn.

Just a few of the factors that worked against us in writing this book were location, communication differences, outside lives, style and pace of work. Our most enjoyable and productive time was the opportunity to physically meet, if only once for a few days, at the beginning of the project. Each of us wanted more of that close time, but living thousands of miles apart did not allow it. We worked with different computers and e-mail systems, so that every time one of us changed, the other had trouble adjusting. Our individual struggles with personal and professional lives took energy away from our work together, at the same time it helped us gain a human empathy and connection with each other. And regarding our style and pace of work? Perhaps Nick put it best at a time of crisis late in the process:

> Because of the way I work, because of my orientation, because of who I am, my way is to be thorough – even obsessional – in collecting the detail, not knowing where I'm going until gradually, ideas emerge . . . I feel this has always placed me at a disadvantage in this project because you work in the opposite fashion, developing broad sweeping ideas, into which you then place the relevant points. This means, of course, you've got a plan while I'm still in the mire!

In short, although we both produced sound work, we did so through very different means. This meant that what we produced was far more difficult to blend than we had ever anticipated.

What, then, were those things that held us together in a productive relationship when our differences could so easily have dissolved our partnership or made it unproductive? Respect was one strong component because we believed that each of us thought effectively and knew our subjects well, even if we approached them in very diverse ways. A work ethic was also key and we wound up writing nearly two books' worth of material in the struggle to find an acceptable meeting place for this one! Furthermore, compromise and patience were essential, as we sought a book where we could blend our ideas while also allowing important differences to have their place. Finally, perhaps personal and professional motivation to complete a major task held us together as much as anything.

In the end, two therapists/authors struggled to overcome numerous blocks based on theoretical and individual differences, as well as on environmental circumstances, to create a book about the core conditions that facilitate all therapy. It has been a very personal, human struggle that is very much like the struggle between therapist and client as they seek to find ways to blend and adjust to their differences. The result is that this book will ask a similar question about the therapeutic environment that we wound up asking about ourselves as therapist/authors: *What conditions hold client and therapist together in productive ways when so many factors promote the downfall of the relationship?*

C H A P T E R   1

Somehow therapy works: core conditions of the facilitative therapeutic environment

RICHARD HAZLER

What conditions hold client and therapist together in productive ways when so many factors promote the downfall of the relationship?

Core conditions

There is a body of theoretical, research and practice information pointing to core conditions that facilitate all therapy. Sometimes, these conditions are more difficult to recognize or produce than at others, as the following interaction between client and therapist exemplifies:[1]*

> I knew nothing of Kristin when she came to see me for our first encounter. She was a young, tall, gangly Scot with an agitated, taut, slightly aggressive air. I tensed as soon as she came through the door. I became even more uneasy when, after briefly scanning the room, she announced – to herself, I think, more than me – 'I'm going to move this'. With this, she picked up the chair – the one which clients usually use – and, turning it round so that it faced the door through which she had just entered, sat down.
>
> With baggy cagoule still zipped up to her chin, Kristin sat low in the chair so that only the back of her head was visible to me. We sat in silence; a long uncomfortable silence as, warily, I waited for what might come next. At last she spoke.

*Superscript numerals refer to numbered notes at the end of the text.

'I want someone to be a witness to my journey. I've seen three counsellors already in the last two weeks and none of them were any good. The last one I only stayed with ten minutes.'

The warning was clear. Most likely, I too would be inadequate to the task. It was as if I were being prepared for something awful. And it was clear that I'd be quickly rejected if I didn't have just the right response. Again a long silence. Again I felt my stomach tighten. What next?

Suddenly, deliberately, she asked me a direct question. 'Are you frightened?' she said.

The truth is the therapist *was* frightened. Or at least he felt something akin to fear. Yet what should he have done? What would have been the best, the most therapeutic approach to take? To be clear and open and admit the fear? To try and explain it perhaps? Or to hide the fact, either by denial or by using words like 'anxiety' and 'frustration', thus giving a whiff of honesty while still keeping appearance of composure properly intact? And then there are other questions, such as whether to take control by moving around to face her directly or whether simply to follow her lead and talk to the back of her head? Maybe it would have been best to have questioned her as to why she wanted to know if the therapist was frightened? Or should the therapist have stayed stonily silent, waiting for her to provide more material for therapeutic use?

Forget for a moment what therapeutic orientation tells you about this woman's problem or the relief you might feel that this therapist is not you. Consider instead what has happened to the environment. The therapist placed chairs to face each other and the client immediately showed a preference for talking to the door. The session was to be about the client, but the client quickly changed the focus to the therapist's anxiety. Although a degree of dis-ease and anxiety is something therapists are likely to feel at times in their relationships with clients – and this they need to be able to bear – they also need to feel comfortable enough to maintain their role. But could a therapist do so here? Indeed, can therapy continue? And if it can, what are the chances for success? Does the therapist need to rearrange the physical, emotional and content characteristics of the environment if he is to secure a successful continuance or is it preferable to make the best of the client's own disruptive choices and, for the moment, leave things as they are?

The issues being raised here are, first, what are the basic environmental conditions necessary for therapy to take place and, second, what are the environmental conditions which best facilitate the therapeutic process? Major aspects of the facilitative environment are often taken for granted as we focus on the principles and techniques of our unique theoretical orientations. Situations like this one help us to realize the importance of, and complexity involved in, creating and maintaining a facilitative environment as the foundation for therapy. The therapeutic techniques we practise do not exist in a vacuum, but demand a facilitative environment in which they can work effectively. An exploration of the characteristics and dynamics involved in creating and maintaining such a facilitative environment form the basis of this book.

Drawing on extensive research and clinical practice from many theoretical perspectives, we examine what constitutes the *core conditions for facilitating therapy*. Comparisons between theories attest to striking differences as well as striking commonalties. Clear and accurate descriptions of concepts and their implementation serve to highlight 'common factors', while those instances where theoretical orientation prompts divergence are specifically identified.

Therapists are not automatically graced with productive therapeutic environments, no matter how advanced their training. No amount of knowledge or experience can dictate all the human factors clients and therapists bring to a given session. Conscious planning and preparation of an environment is the starting place, but the ability to recognize and adapt to changing situations is essential follow-up. The conceptual guides and practical examples that follow are designed to aid understanding of the core facilitating conditions essential for therapeutic efficacy and to offer direction for implementing them in the real world of therapeutic practice.

Success across therapies

Perhaps the best descriptor of core conditions is that they pertain, in some general way, to conditions that promote productive interactions between therapist and client. All therapy requires some form of connection, although we may disagree on what combination of physical (visual, tactile, olfactory, etc.), verbal, written, spiritual or other conditions are essential to promote that connection. Even though a gathering of experienced therapists would produce a wide variety of ways to visualize and deal with Kristin, research and practice confirm that each therapist would probably be successful.

The chances of Kristin being helped by an experienced therapist are quite good. Meta-analyses of research studies on the value of psychotherapy find that from two-thirds to four-fifths of people do get better as a result of therapy. These same analyses show that the theoretical approach of a therapist does not seem to make any consistent difference (Hunt 1993). Jerome and Julia Frank (1991) probably best capture the way many professionals see these results in practice when they conclude that theories which endure rather than disappear must be doing some good or people would stop going to therapists of those theoretical orientations. Even studies done by groups evaluating the profession from the outside have determined that therapy works (*Consumer Reports* 1995). These findings are good news for the public, but they also cause headaches for therapists and educators trying to determine best techniques or even attempting to define the key factors in quality practice.

What can account for consistently positive therapeutic results coming from such a wide variety of theoretical approaches? Garfield and Bergin (1994) summarize the findings and thoughts of many in determining that there must be some common or 'non-specific' conditions that all 'quality' therapists provide. Identifying these facilitative conditions has been difficult, but one consistent theme throughout the research is that a significant part of the answer lies within what is generally called the 'therapeutic relationship' (Luborsky *et al.* 1988; Beutler *et al.* 1994).

The relationship factor

Therapists who consider working with someone like Kristin have good reason to be concerned about the potential for poor outcomes. All of a therapist's training, experience and theoretical knowledge cannot make up for an environment that denies the development of productive interactions. The question is, what facilitative conditions promote a positive relationship?

The past 40 years of research on therapy outcomes has shown us the importance of the relationship in general. The critical specifics of this relationship have been harder to identify, but some progress has been made, as Luborsky's (1994) review of this research shows. One essential ingredient is that clients must have some capacity for a positive relationship. Those with better mental health are more likely to demonstrate this capacity and those who are making progress with a therapist tend to continue improving on this capacity and its benefits. In effect, it appears that the healthier clients are at the beginning of therapy or the better they become during therapy, the more likely they are to develop the necessary therapeutic relationships.

The same research shows that therapists have the ability to improve the positive relationship capacity of their clients. Emphasizing behaviours that focus on the relationship between client and therapist seems to be the general way that such a positive relational environment is promoted. Dealing with client defences, guilt and problematic feelings towards the therapist are all effective measures a therapist can take. Therapists may not be able to control the entire relational environment, but it appears that they must at least work towards a point where the relationship is 'good enough' to be therapeutic (Horvath and Greenberg 1994).

Kristin brings much less capacity for positive relationships than a therapist might like. The question is, does she bring enough to begin making progress? Her therapist must somehow judge this potential and then behave in ways that create a facilitative environment where a more productive relationship can evolve. Theory, practice and research each provide their own pieces of information on the dimensions of a facilitative environment that help direct what therapists can do to maximize the potential for a positive therapeutic relationship and thus therapeutic success.

Environmental factors

Kristin may be physically in the therapy room but how much is she invested in being there? What can cause such problematic situations? What psychological, emotional and/or social factors do such situations reflect? How intransigent are these problems and what, if anything, can be done to provide an environment that will best overcome them and enable therapy to progress? Therapists will need to make judgements on all these questions as they try to determine whether to see a client like Kristin and under what conditions.

The information available on the connection between facilitative environment – in particular, the therapeutic relationship – and successful therapy is multidimensional. Each dimension provides a separate focus and details that must first be considered individually to make them clear and useful as part of the whole. No single dimension fully controls the relationship, although differing views of theory, research and practice apportion widely varying importance to the different factors involved.

Involvement

Conditions that produce some form of involvement are needed between client and therapist for the therapist to take partial responsibility for any positive developments. Being physically in the same room is the common contact for most therapies, but even that is challenged by increasing numbers of professionals who are doing therapy over the telephone or Internet (Greeno *et al.* 1997). Moderate temperature and lighting, comfortable sitting or reclining opportunities rather than standing and minimized distracting noises, clutter and interruptions are found in virtually any successful therapist's room. These essentials are so much a part of the professional atmosphere that they are virtually taken for granted in textbooks and research. Yet theoretical differences regarding the physical foundations of therapy already begin to emerge within these basic boundaries.

The classical analyst has a client/patient lie on a couch, unable to see the therapist so that the client's thinking might be relatively uninfluenced by the therapist's physical presence. Gestalt therapists, at the other end of the spectrum, consider essential therapeutic ingredients to be close, face-to-face, person-to-person, even physical contact. Each theory thus has its own unique view of what physical behaviours are appropriate in relation to the purpose, techniques and goals of therapy.

Emotions

All therapies attend to emotions. The difference is in the value placed on emotions and their role in therapy. Person-centred therapists attend directly to client emotions as a vehicle for understanding the unique aspects of their phenomenological worlds. Their belief is that logic, reason, history, and so on, used alone draw attention away from the most unique experiences of clients, while emotions are more likely to highlight these important aspects. Most cognitive therapists, on the other hand, advocate that thought, logic and illogic control emotions and that the emphasis of therapy should therefore be on those 'rational' processes. Similarly, classical behavioural therapists will use learning and training to change emotions, which they see as being little more than secondary markers of behaviours.

Culture

Society and cultures imbue therapists and clients with expectations that must be given attention for therapy to succeed. White Europeans and Americans have had the greatest influence on the development of most therapeutic/counselling theories. Katz (1985: 619) summarizes this fact by stating, 'similarities between white culture and cultural values that form the foundations of traditional counseling theory and practice exist and are interchangeable'. Feminist (Weiner and Boss 1985; Elliott 1999) and multicultural (Pedersen 1994; Parham 1996) criticisms of these theories are generally based on the concept that not everyone fits this male, Euro-American worldview. Asian cultures, for example, would place more value on the family or group identity than on individuality. Females also tend to take a more collaborative approach to life than males. On a societal level, some would encourage therapists to report anyone with anti-government thinking, while others would see even plotting and planning as therapeutically private issues unless they were likely to physically harm someone. These few examples highlight the need to take cultural factors into consideration in developing a facilitative environment.

Thought

What people think, how they arrive at those thoughts and what they can do about them take up much of the time and energy in the therapeutic environment. Questions about people's ability to think or style of thinking need to be considered, since theories vary on the extent and type of thinking necessary. Dealing with ambiguity and abstractions are essentials for the client in existential therapy, whereas the same client working with a behavioural therapist would be given much more simplistic and concrete thinking tasks. Adlerians, on the other hand, would ask clients to do substantial memory work about their childhood with the expectation that such memories could and would be recalled.

Some theories presume that sufficient recall of information and perceptions are available in the conscious mind for therapy to work. Others spend more time attempting to illuminate the unconscious with the belief that key therapeutic factors are not available to simple conscious recall. Techniques used vary between therapists as they view the thinking process and abilities of their clients differently, even though they all attend to the importance of the thinking variable in one way or another.

Time

The past provides the greatest number of actual events for consideration in therapy. The present provides the most immediately available and tangible events. The future holds the much-desired, imagined events that might constitute a better existence, although there is nothing concrete or observable about them. All theories attend to each of these three time frames in their own ways, while they also have different priorities as to which frame deserves greater attention.

The 'here-and-now' focus of gestalt and other humanistic oriented therapies demonstrate an orientation to therapy that emphasizes immediate interaction and change. *What is done is done and what will happen in the future is fully dependent on what we do now. So concentrate on the present.* In contrast, psychodynamic and behavioural therapists, who disagree on many areas, both emphasize that the present is built upon the past. They give great attention to the past for the sake of understanding: *Only after it is understood how the present came about, can you move to change the present and future in selective ways.* Common to all therapies, though, is the assumption that an improved future results from some change occurrence. Yet, whether that change results from the formal planning characteristic of a behavioural therapy or the natural evolution of adjustments based on a better understanding of the past characteristic of a psychodynamic approach remains open to debate.

The above dimensions of a facilitative environment form a framework in which the core facilitative conditions essential for therapy exist. Once those conditions, which are the subject of this book, are recognized, direct actions can be taken to maintain positive conditions, address weak ones and delay or speed up the pace of the therapy to make use of those times when the most viable conditions are available.

Conditions versus techniques

One problem that arises when considering core facilitative conditions is differentiating between the conditions and actions that produce a facilitative environment, and the therapeutic techniques that require such an environment in order to be effective. Therapeutic techniques and the development of core conditions are often interwoven in most discussions of theoretical approaches, with the conditions getting little direct attention. This book seeks to clarify the distinction between conditions and techniques and, by focusing upon the former, go some way to addressing the theoretical neglect and redressing the balance.

The debate about what qualifies as a facilitative condition and what is a therapeutic technique is a live one. Indeed, it is a debate that is evidenced in the chapters that follow. While a cleaner and more uniform answer than the one this book offers might be desirable, such uniformity simply does not reflect the current state of the profession.

Variations on a theme of success

A clear theme throughout the literature is that therapy works and those who practise effective therapy can be recognized. Obviously, we do not have a final answer to exactly what good therapy is or we would only study that 'one correct approach'. The pieces that unite therapeutic variations must be found within the philosophies, assumptions, history, techniques, research and conclusions drawn by different theories of psychotherapy.

The next three chapters explore the successful therapeutic variations through three broad theoretical frameworks: psychodynamic (Chapter 2), cognitive/behavioural (Chapter 3) and existential/humanistic (Chapter 4). These three chapters make up the bulk of the text. They examine the philosophical perspectives and psychological paradigms upon which each of these three therapeutic schools is based and explore the core conditions which, according to these paradigms and perspectives, are deemed essential for therapeutic efficacy.

The final chapter focuses briefly upon the commonalties and differences between the core facilitative conditions across theoretical viewpoints. The chapter's format – a dialogue between therapists/authors – is designed to communicate both shared conclusions and separate slants on those conclusions. It is a format that reflects the current state of therapeutic thinking, in which a growing recognition of commonalties is accompanied by a strong allegiance to different perspectives and a resulting awareness of some striking differences in terms of emphasis and nuance.

C H A P T E R   **2**

Core conditions of the psychodynamic environment

NICK BARWICK

Introduction: an environmental paradox

Kristin asked whether the therapist was frightened. In doing so, she was trying to find out about an environmental condition with which she was hesitantly engaging: the condition of the therapist's mind. A reasonable desire. Yet faced with this question, most psychodynamic therapists would not 'tell'. Such 'reserve' tends to evoke **frustration**, and frustration is a core condition of the psychodynamic environment.

Ironically, frustration also threatens therapy. Most patients want something – an answer to a question, a solution to a problem, love. If continually refused **gratification**, there may come a point when they feel it simply isn't worth the pain. Thus we are presented with a curious environmental paradox, where core conditions of frustration and gratification both seem to have their place.

Paradigms and perspectives

This paradox betrays a controversy: two views about the source of psychological distress. One, a drive-discharge view, sees the source as primarily internal – the conflict-ridden 'nature' of the human psyche in which each individual 'struggles with lasting urges'/instincts/drives (Pine 1990); the other, a relational view, sees it as primarily external – the environment's failure to provide conditions necessary for the 'nurture' of what is essentially a relationship-seeking organism.

Therapies founded on the drive-discharge paradigm (e.g. Freudian, Ego Psychology) aim to help patients gain insight into their instinctual, conflict-ridden, internal world. Insight's purpose is to free patients from control of unconscious forces, enabling them to manage innate conflicts better and more effectively forge their own destinies (Freud [1923a] 1991). Therapies based on the relational paradigm (e.g. Object Relations,[1] Self Psychology) seek to ameliorate the harmful impact of early environmental failures. Although the psychology of internal conflict and the import of insight are rarely abandoned, the focus shifts to the therapeutic relationship and its attempt to make developmental redress.

These paradigms inform a therapist's understanding of what kind of environment best facilitates the therapeutic process. They suggest a recipe of what conditions, in what proportions, create the richest environmental mix. For therapists endeavouring to help patients manage innate conflicts, conditions of frustration are favoured. For therapists focusing on developmental deficit, conditions offering gratification are preferred.

Core conditions

The analytic setting: a theatre for transference operations

The **analytic setting** *is* the environment – the physical, temporal and relational place where therapy occurs. Freudian therapy occurs in an environment analogous to an operating theatre. The theatre is sterilized and the therapist, adopting the role of 'surgeon . . . puts aside all his feeling, even his human sympathy', and focuses entirely upon 'performing the operation as skilfully as possible' (Freud [1912a] 1958: 115). Ironically, this attitude stems not from a denial of the import of emotional experience, but from a recognition. This recognition lies at the heart of the use of the **transference** (see Grant and Crawley, forthcoming).

Transference, the emotionally charged re-playing of past relationships in the present, offers for scrutiny a living re-enactment of early traumas. Although dubbed 'the most powerful therapeutic instrument' (Freud [1923b] 1955: 247), it threatens to undermine therapy as well as offer 'cure'. After all, simply to repeat destructive relationships hardly moves a patient forward. For transference to be of use, not only must it be established but it must also be maintained, managed and, ultimately, dissolved. In Freudian therapy, the process of establishing, maintaining and to some extent managing the transference, is a principal use to which the analytic setting is put.

Transference happens everywhere. However, a particularly virulent strain of transference, the transference neurosis, is stimulated in therapy as a result of **regression**. Regression – a 'harking back to older psychical structures' and more 'primitive [infantile] methods of expression' (Freud [1900/1914] 1976: 699) – tends to emerge in an environment which frustrates the patient's quest for gratification. Therapist **abstinence** – a refusal to satisfy patient demands or fulfil roles the patient would impose – serves exactly this frustrating function (Freud [1915] 1958). Indeed, abstinence may even be equated with 'reinstating' suffering (Freud [1919] 1955). Together, abstinence and the 'motivating' condition of suffering contribute to the necessary condition of **optimal deprivation** (Greenson 1967).

It is not only abstention that stimulates regression. The setting's physical and temporal aspects impact too. For example, **frequency** and **length of sessions** – in full analysis, five times a week for 50 minutes a time – encourages emotional intensity, while the use of **couch** with patient reclined, physically restricted and without easy access to visual contact, emphasizes the encounter's inequality (see Moraitis 1995). Together, these conditions echo early mother–infant relationships (Spitz 1956). The infant role is further enhanced by the patient's practice of **free association** – talk which is as free and uninhibited as possible. This invites regression to primary process (primitive ways of thinking) and dream (Macalpine 1950; Lewin 1955), while the activity itself resembles the indescriminatory prattling of a child (Spitz 1956, cited in Greenson 1967).

Reserve
In Freudian therapy, the maintenance of the transference is a matter of keeping the operating theatre clean. The presence of any material, other than the patient's, threatens 'contamination'. Thus, all elements of the 'real' are purged.

The most important reality to purge is the personality of the therapist. At the outset, he is **anonymous** and he tries to keep it this way. He refrains from educative or therapeutic 'ambition' (Freud [1912a] 1958), adopting instead a strictly non-directive approach. 'Opaque', like a **mirror**, he shows 'nothing but what is shown to him' (Freud [1912a] 1958: 117). Controlling his emotions, he 'blankets' his personality and, like the surgeon, scrubs himself clean.

One source of contamination the therapist needs to guard against is the **counter-transference** (Jacobs and Rowan, forthcoming). This refers both to the therapist's own transference and to his unconscious reaction to that of the patient (Freud [1910] 1959). Freud ([1914] 1958) saw the need to keep this 'in check'; refraining from bringing in his own agenda and from getting drawn into the patient's relational game. Indeed, the danger of counter-transference infestation is one reason for the therapist's own therapy. Self-awareness provides a better chance of acting with **restraint**. Abstinence, anonymity and counter-transference restraint are all aspects of therapist **reserve**, which, together, constitute the principal condition of **behavioural neutrality** (Franklin 1990).

Out of the purging process sustained by behavioural neutrality, the therapist emerges as **blank screen** (Freud [1913] 1958). Upon the screen, all patient unconscious phantasies are projected. Projected, they are scrutinized with 'non-selective', 'flexible', 'dis-interested', 'unbiased', **evenly suspended attention**. Without this 'the physician is in danger of never finding anything but what he already knows'. Evenly suspended attention thus describes a mental poise that matches patient free association, ensuring that the therapist refrains from 'substituting a censorship of his own' for the one 'the patient has foregone' (Freud [1912a] 1958: 111–17). This further aspect of reserve is usefully embraced by the term **attitudinal neutrality** (Franklin 1990), a condition in which the therapist is 'non-judgemental', since he neither takes sides nor has favourites both in relation to the patient's intrapsychic struggles (i.e. between id, super ego and defensive ego; see A. Freud [1936] 1992) and to significant others. The irony is that in an environment apparently stripped of a 'real relationship' – a direct and genuine personal relationship relatively uncontaminated by transference distortions (see Greenson 1967) – the therapist becomes an instrument for an intimate knowing (see Russell 1996).

Tact

Freud's rules are mainly prohibitions. In contrast, Ferenczi ([1928] 1980) suggests a number of 'shoulds'. **Tact**, for example, is a 'should' founded upon empathy. The therapist intuits when to speak, when to interpret and when to say nothing at all. The intention is to guard against 'unnecessarily stimulating the patient's resistance' (Ferenczi [1928] 1980: 90) and giving the patient the unconsciously deeply desired opportunity for withdrawal. Tact thus modifies conditions of frustration, abstinence and behavioural and attitudinal neutrality in an effort to keep the patient at work. The therapist should not give way to the patient, but rather achieve an **elasticity** in which, while pulling in his own direction, he 'yield[s] to the patient's pull' (p. 95).

Tact is an essential condition in the Freudian environment. Its import is evident in qualifying phrases such as **compassionate neutrality** (Greenson 1958; Weigert 1970), **benevolent neutrality** and

neutrality with an affirmative tone (Stone 1961). Yet Ferenczi
([1930] 1980) goes further, advocating conditions that have been
less well received. With some patients, he suggests that the trauma
re-experienced in the transference, rather than offering reflective
opportunity, threatens to re-traumatize. Although not dismissing
the motivational need for suffering, he sees **economy of suffering**
as more apt. To this end, he proposes counterbalancing the condition of frustration with the condition of **indulgence**.
The condition of indulgence gratifies. It sanctions displays of affection:
holding patients' hands, accompanying them on walks, on holidays,
hugging, kissing. Considering it 'natural and appropriate . . . for the
doctor to be sincerely a feeling person, at times empathically sympath-
izing, at times openly irritated' (Ferenczi [1932] 1980, cited in Russell
1996), Ferenczi advocates self-disclosure even to the point of allowing
patients to place *him* on the couch. This reciprocity, referred to as
mutual analysis, Ferenczi considers potentially helpful at times of
therapeutic impasse, although it is to be a technique 'of last resort'
(Dupont 1988).

Freud's abandonment of 'seduction theory' had led to an emphasis
on internal conflicts. In contrast, Ferenczi focused increasingly on
the impact of real trauma in his patients' lives. Regarding patients as
victims of insensitive parenting, he felt their need 'to be adopted
and to partake for the first time . . . of the advantages of a normal
nursery' (Ferenczi [1930] 1980: 124). Thus the 'nursery' becomes not
only the place where trauma can be remembered, but the method
by which it can be relieved (Hoffer 1990). In a phrase attributed to
Ferenzci, 'It is the physician's love that heals the patient'.[2]

Order
A less dramatic transference-management method is to attend to the
frame (Milner 1952). This refers to the boundaried space of the setting
that provides an 'area of illusion' in which 'symbolic discourse can
actualize' (Khan 1974: 252). Fundamental here is the **fixed-frame**:
the conditions of total privacy, predictability and consistency in
terms of place, time, frequency and fees, and total confidentiality
(Langs 1988). As well as maintaining therapist anonymity and conveying neutrality, the frame offers patients stability, contributing to
feelings of security essential for therapeutic work. Indeed, only with
the frame's ground and ground rules established can the patient feel
safe enough to participate in free associative play.[3]

Not only must the therapist protect the frame from external intrusions but from attacks from within. Most patients, for example, try

to pressure the therapist to modify the frame. However, to gratify these pressures can aggravate the very dis-ease from which the patient seeks relief (Bleger 1967). For instance, to offer reduced fees can feed narcissistic tendencies (Kron 1971) or enforce feelings of being in another's debt. So can the waiving of fees for missed sessions (Freud [1913] 1958). Similarly, although an argument can be made for extending the 'hour' at points of crisis (Jacobson 1993), this may be at longer-term therapeutic cost (Meissner 1996). In fact, any lack of firm frame management can imply unhelpful weaknesses on the therapist's part (Haak 1957). Certainly, Langs (1975a, 1980) sees fixed-frame deviations (as opposed to other frame deviations such as erroneous interpretations and non-interpretative interventions) as the most disruptive, leading to transference gratification and countertransference disarray. Thus, although patients may resent firm frame management, they may find reassurance in the fact that their therapist cannot be overwhelmed, manipulated or seduced (Langs 1974).

Personal involvement
Related to concerns regarding re-traumatization are criticisms that a preoccupation with anonymity can 'suffocate' patient, therapist and therapeutic process (Coltart 1992); that the 'principle' of abstention, too often becoming a rigid 'rule' (Fox 1984), may feel controlling (Lomas 1987); that behavioural and attitudinal neutrality may feel punitively critical (Treurniet 1993) and invalidating (Wachtel 1986); that deprivation in a secure frame may promote both undue suffering (Strupp 1973) and patient compliance (Meissner 1996). Further criticism centres on the assumption that a therapist can eliminate his or her real self. Although reticent neutrality promotes an attitude of objectivity, it is a contemporary truism that objectivity is not absolute. Every experiment is influenced by the experimenter and every observation by the person who observes. Thus therapists are **participant-observers** (Sullivan 1954) and although silence, behavioural and attitudinal neutrality, even technical correctness may appear objective, not only are they inevitably invested with the personality of the therapist (Peterfreund 1983; Schafer 1983), but to ignore this fact is to ignore the therapist's capacity to exploit them to his or her own transference ends (Jacobs 1991). It is the recognition of therapists' interpersonal involvement with their patients and the decision to utilize this interaction to therapeutic effect that distinguishes two-person psychological therapies based on the relational paradigm from one-person psychological therapies based on the drive-discharge one. Many therapists, therefore, seeing their real presence as an inevit-

able condition of the environment, concede that no matter how anonymous they try to be, they will inevitably proffer real aspects of themselves just as patients will inevitably tease out real clues. In fact, to enforce anonymity can unhelpfully contribute to therapist authority and power (Renik 1995; Gelso and Hayes 1998). Thus, since a central aim of therapy is to liberate the individual from compliance (Freud [1919] 1955, [1937] 1964), therapist anonymity can be seen to be therapeutically counterproductive (Benjamin 1994).[4]

Langs (1978) sees the therapist's unconscious intrusion into the environment as commonplace, but unhelpful. Therapist counter-transference continually contaminates, violating the very frame the therapist tries to maintain. Since an intact frame is essential for therapeutic work, he concludes that much of the therapist's attention must be on ways of addressing and redressing these violations.

For Gill (1982a,b, 1988), even trying to keep the frame intact and theatre clean is wasted effort – contagion is everywhere. The 'blank screen' is 'illusion', not only because the therapist's personality permeates his or her interventions (Peters 1991) but because patient's and therapist's conscious and unconscious responses inevitably interact. This view of an interactional and intersubjective environment reconceptualizes transference as the patient's response to therapist cues to which the former then gives meaning. Furthermore, it shifts the role of therapist from objectively observing authority figure to participating collaborator. The therapeutic process thus becomes one in which, together, both patient and therapist must try to make sense of their interactions (Stolorow *et al.* 1994; Trop and Stolorow 1997). In such collaborative conditions, abstinence, anonymity and behavioural and attitudinal neutrality may, at well-chosen times, be abandoned and counter-transference disclosure advocated, not just as a means of overcoming therapeutic impasse (Maroda 1991), but, through **direct affective engagement**, of adding a new dimension to analytic interaction (Ehrenberg 1984) and of confirming the egalitarian nature of the joint effort to understand and to learn (Ehrenberg 1992; Schacter 1994, 1995). The therapeutic attitude consistent with this form of engagement has been termed **interactional neutrality**: a 'flexible attitude' in which the therapist brings into play 'any aspect of his relatedness to the patient that fosters the patient's self-expression' in the task of exploration and self-understanding (Franklin 1990: 213).[5]

Of course, there are good reasons for paying heed to Freud's more conservative 'recommendations'. A cautious orthodoxy helps protect the patient and keeps the therapist in professional check. This is clearly so when it comes to the danger of a therapist acting out his or her own narcissistic needs (Schafer [1983] 1993). An **atmosphere of safety** is an essential condition if the patient is to risk fruitful engagement. The therapist's capacity to remain proof against a whole range of temptations provides the best evidence that a belief in such safety is well met.

Nevertheless, there may be some non-therapeutic reasons for Freud's exhortations: his desire to make his fledgling discipline scientifically credible; the influence on his thinking of the Protestant suspicion of pleasure and gratification; the prevalent masculine view of 'professional' work – distant and exact (Lomas 1987). And then there was Breuer (Freud and Breuer [1895] 1991). Reeling from patient accusations – apparently false – of sexual misconduct, Breuer fled psychoanalysis altogether. Guarding against psychic infection, then, is all very understandable, yet the fear of the incendiary potential of this most peculiarly intimate of dyads may have prompted a medical environment more 'antiseptic' than clean (Winer 1994).

Equality
The notion of a more egalitarian environment is one that has long been familiar to Jungians. This is, in part, because the Jungian view of the psyche includes the concept of the 'collective unconscious'. This 'unconscious', in contrast to its personal counterpart, alludes to humanity's (and thus both patient's and therapist's) shared heritage of predispositions and potentialities – 'archetypes' – awaiting to be fleshed out by individual experience. Rather than focusing on the transference (often the manifestation of the patient's personal unconscious), Classical Jungian therapists attend more to the manifestations of the collective unconscious – 'archetypal images' – for example, as in dreams. This is because, for Classical Jungians, it is the patients' growing awareness of the archetypal dimensions of their lives that enables them to become more fully themselves: whole, indivisible, distinct from, yet related to, other people and the collective psychology. It follows that Classical Jungian therapists seek to foster an environment that facilitates the emergence of archetypal material and its creative utilization in the natural transformative process of becoming: of 'individuation'.

The relational environment most appropriate to the facilitation of this process is characterized by the condition of **equality**.[6] This is a complex notion but one that gives subtle resonance to Jung's remark to one patient, 'So you're in the soup too!' (Bennet 1982: 32). Elaborating on the concept, Jung referred to therapy as a 'dialectical process' and to the relationship as one of **dialectical mutuality**. In practice, this means that the therapist is far less reserved and far more active than in Freudian therapy, 'amplifying', where appropriate, the patient's associations with his own fund of knowledge (Adler 1966). The mutuality of therapist–patient interchange is further apparent in the use of two chairs – as opposed to chair and couch – which, rather than promoting dependency, promotes the experience of a collaborative venture in which therapist and patient work as colleagues on a shared task.[7] Patient dependency is further mitigated by offering therapy less frequently (once or twice weekly) and by incorporating significant breaks. Complementing this, personal work on dreams outside the therapy session serves to heighten the patient's sense of responsibility for the process.

The therapist's own condition as **wounded healer** is an essential aspect of an environment of equality. Although initially therapists may identify their own wounded aspects in their patients – thus establishing an emotional knowledge of them – and patients may identify their healing capacities in the therapist – thus establishing a trust in the therapist's capacity to heal – the goal is for these identifications eventually to be owned (see Guggenbühl-Craig 1971; Groesbeck 1975; Samuels 1985). Ownership and the therapist's utilization of his or her condition of wounded healer is one reason for Jung's insistence on the therapist's own therapy. Since it is the therapist that is the 'instrument' of therapy (Jung [1963] 1977), it is the therapist's 'own hurt that gives the measure of his power to heal' (Jung [1954] 1966, CW 16: para. 239).

The importance of a training therapy is particularly crucial, since Jungians extend the notion of equality and 'mutuality' to mutual transformation. Indeed, Jung ([1954] 1966) went as far as to suggest that the therapist was 'in analysis' just as much as the patient. The success of therapy thus depends upon the raw material ('prima materia') which both patient and therapist bring to the containing vessel of the structured therapeutic situation (i.e. the **vas**) and the kind of mutual transformation/'transmutation' that occurs within the 'vas', through the 'heat' or 'fermentatio' of the interaction.

Jung's use of alchemical metaphors may seem distant and arcane. However, the demands the alchemical process places on the therapist are not. Since the process depends on interaction of 'two psychic wholes' – the two personalities of the participants – the 'doctor must emerge from his anonymity and give an account of himself, just as he expects his patients to do' (Jung [1954] 1966: para. 23). The emphasis here is on a mutuality of 'feeling'. Without a **feeling relationship** there can be no 'coniunctio' – the chemical combining or mating of unlike substances/'opposites'. Without coniunctio, there can be no transformation.

The feeling relationship, particularly in terms of patient–therapist direct unconscious communications, is linked to Jung's view of counter-transference. Although Jung ([1954] 1966) recognized the possibility of 'psychic infection' and the danger of therapist identifying with patient (para. 358), he also saw the counter-transference as an 'important organ of information' (para. 163; see also Fordham [1960] 1974). The countertransference is evidence of the patient's unconscious attempts to influence the therapist – the transference – and it is by being 'susceptible to influence' that the therapist may 'influence' and guide the patient (Jung [1954] 1966, CW XVI: para. 163). The influence the therapist seeks to have on the patient, however, should promote balanced 'adaptation' – an essential aspect of individuation – rather than one-sided distortion, and this is another reason for the rigour of the therapist's therapy. Thus the relationship may better be described as one of **asymmetrical mutuality**, since it has much in common with the teacher–student relationship or, more aptly, perhaps that of mother and child (see Samuels 1985).

Jung's emphasis on mutuality can thus be seen to lead in two directions, each of which is accompanied by its own version of an optimal therapeutic environment. For those Jungian therapists (Classical and Archetypal Schools) who focus primarily on content (e.g. dreams and other manifestations of the unconscious), the collaborative characteristics of the condition of mutuality ally it with the environment recommended by Ego Psychology, namely the 'alliance' (see below). For those Jungians (Developmental School; see Fordham 1957) who focus on process (i.e. the feeling relationship between therapist and patient), the mother–child characteristics of asymmetrical mutuality ally it with the relational environment advocated by object relations therapy, in particular the environmental conditions of 'containment' and 'holding' (see below). Because of this, Jungians of the Developmental School prefer couch to chair, more frequent rather than less frequent sessions and a more reserved rather than more active therapist role.

*Adding to the analytic setting: a consulting room for
alliance collaborations*

The alliance
The **alliance** is a collaborative aspect of the therapeutic relationship. Its purpose is to keep the patient attached to therapist and therapy,

and to enable him or her to reflect. It is both cognitive and affective in nature, rational and irrational.

The concept of a rational alliance is rooted in Freud's ([1923a] 1991) structural model of the mind – ego, superego and id. Against the id's instinctual and the superego's conscientious demands, the therapist forms a 'pact' (Freud [1937] 1964, [1940] 1993): a pact with the patient's 'mature' ego. Ego Psychology suggests the mature ego represents a set of ego functions that are 'autonomous', that is, free from the influence of instincts (Hartmann 1939). This gives credence to an aspect of the therapeutic environment free from transference: a consulting room, annexed to the operating theatre, in which rational, collaborative, patient–therapist exchanges can occur. The **ego alliance** (Sterba 1934) describes such a dialogue within such a 'room'.

The ego alliance is rooted in patient–therapist unity of purpose – the struggle towards health. It relies upon the patient's 'observant ego' identifying with the analysing function of the therapist. The therapist's task is to encourage a separation of observant and transference-laden 'experiencing ego', to encourage a **therapeutic split**.

The **therapeutic alliance** (Zetzel [1956] 1987) also emphasizes rational aspects and the need for a therapeutic split. It posits a 'stable relationship' which provides both a 'barrier' to uncontrolled ego regression and a safe reality 'against which the fantasies, memories, and emotions evoked by the transference neurosis can be measured, contrasted' (Zetzel [1958] 1987: 185) and managed. In the process, it advocates a less sterilized interaction. The therapist takes on the role of more personalized partner who offers, through his or her 'real' presence, an important parent-like object with whom the patient can positively identify (Zetzel [1970] 1987).

The **working alliance** (Greenson 1965) also provides a transference-managing function: keeping the patient in therapy, even when the transference-trauma prompts him to give up. Firmly based in the 'real relationship', it gives the therapist licence to offer **appropriate gratifications** (Stone 1961) to counterbalance 'optimal deprivation'. Such gratifications are proffered, in part, by the therapist's consultative approach. The therapist outlines procedures, explains techniques, discusses 'real problems'. It is proffered too by therapist 'humaneness' – 'compassion', 'concern', 'respect for the individual' and 'therapeutic intent' (Greenson 1965). As with the therapeutic alliance, these conditions modify those of abstinence, neutrality and frustration. Thus the white coat of surgeon is exchanged for the less sterile cloth of consultant's suit.

Variations on the alliance concept are legion: 'rational transference' (Fenichel 1941), 'therapeutic contract' (Menninger 1958), 'rational alliance' (Gutheil and Havens 1979), 'realistic bond' (Kohut 1971). All strike the same reasonable note. It is this very reasonableness that attracts debate (Novick 1970). Can the patient's ego really be sufficiently detached from the neurotic personality to be adequately 'observing'? Can the alliance really be free of unconscious forces (Evans 1976) or the consultation room so clearly separated from the transference-ridden theatre of operations itself (Lipton 1977; Brenner 1979; Hanly 1994)?

Neither therapeutic nor working alliance are in fact ignorant of unconscious, irrational, transference presence. Yet such presence is seen as 'friendly', 'positive', 'unobjectionable' (Freud [1912b] 1958). Having its source in affectionate early relationships, the 'attaching' of patient to therapist is viewed as occurring naturally (Freud [1913] 1958) and is 'the vehicle of success in psycho-analysis' (Freud [1912b] 1958: 105), not because it carries curative properties, but because it keeps the therapeutic work on the road.

Attachment-oriented therapists follow a similar line (Bowlby 1988). When patients feel threatened, their natural impulse is to look for an 'attachment figure', a person they consider stronger and wiser than themselves. Once they have established a **secure base** (Ainsworth 1982) with this figure, they can begin to explore the nature of the threat. This healthy **therapeutic attachment** is in line with the friendly, transference-based, therapeutic alliance.

Despite descriptors such as 'mature' (Stone 1961) and 'basic transference' (Greenacre [1968] 1971), some therapists believe that within this therapeutic alliance less palatable transference aspects still lurk. Further, a reified alliance becomes unavailable to psychodynamic scrutiny (Fonagy 1990, cited in Sandler *et al.* 1992) and debilitating transference aspects can easily be missed (Eagle and Wolitzky 1997). Even a **misalliance**, a rampant form of counter-transference infestation, can occur (Langs 1975b).

Sandler *et al.* (1992) usefully summarize the multi-faceted alliance. Their 'narrow definition' is mature ego-based, with shared therapeutic intent at its core. Their 'wider definition' is id-based, and includes unconscious factors that keep the patient in therapy. The relative import of these aspects fluctuate. The ego-based alliance may take precedence at termination; the id-based alliance may dominate at the start. Furthermore, the more disturbed the patient, the greater the import of the alliance and the likelihood that classical conditions may need to be modified by gratifications of a modest type (see Parry and Birkett 1996).

Patient contributions
The conditions necessary for establishing and maintaining the alliance reside in both patient and therapist. Patients must do more than lie back and free associate. They must draw on cognitive, affective, rational, irrational, conscious and unconscious aspects of themselves. Therapists provide conditions to encourage this yet, in the end, certain mental 'pre-conditions' patients themselves must bring. 'Derived from positive experiences in childhood', these preconditions are vital for both 'maintenance of the therapeutic split' and for that 'fondness' for the therapist which assures 'maintenance of a sufficient trust' (Kohut 1971: 207).

Most alliance concepts cite **basic trust** (Erikson 1950) as *the* key patient precondition. Basic trust is an attitude to people which is hopeful and generally optimistic. Founded upon an infant's early experiences of security, it is gained by an internalization of an early 'alliance' between the infant and its *primary object*, usually its mother (Stern 1985). Without it, the alliance is unlikely to be healthy (Horvath and Symonds 1991) and the work of therapy is unlikely to progress (Hani 1973).

There is also a need for **secondary trust** (Mehlman 1976, cited in Meissner 1996). This evolves from the child's willingness to remain open to parental influence. Mehlman suggests early trauma cramps openness, causing children to defensively parent themselves. Premature self-parenting may protect the immediate sense of vulnerability, yet subsequent mental rigidity limits constructive use of parent objects, such as the therapist, later in life.

Other developmentally achieved pre-conditions include **autonomy**, **initiative** and **industry** (Erikson 1950, cited in Meissner 1996). All contribute to the alliance, although their import varies at different stages of the therapeutic process. Thus at commencement, trust is likely to be most important, particularly during regression. Later, basic autonomy is necessary if the patient is to take responsibility. Gradually, initiative and industry are useful and provide confidence for the patient's own interpretative efforts.

The fore-grounding of the patient's contribution to therapy fits well with the shift from a more authoritarian to a more collaborative approach. Yet such fore-grounding also makes considerable demands. True, these developmentally achieved conditions are both brought to therapy and built upon. But what if patient foundations are insufficient for the therapist to be able to build? Without basic trust how can the patient 'attach' (Freud [1913] 1958; Erikson 1950)? Without basic autonomy, how can the patient observe (Freud [1920]

1991; Loewenstein 1972)? Concerns like these have caused some therapists to suggest that some patients do not have the necessary ego strength to form an alliance and thus undertake therapy (Greenson 1965). Others reflect wryly that patients who are truly able to form an alliance are 'a fiction' and, if they existed, they probably would not need treatment at all (Winer 1994)!

Adaptability
The problem of dealing with patients lacking the preconditions for therapy has prompted some therapists to modify **parameters** (Eissler 1953) – conditions of setting and technique – to secure an alliance. For example, Adler (1985), recognizing the inability of more disturbed patients to call on soothing memories to maintain a 'stable relationship', modifies abstinence by emphasizing the reality of his continued presence and care. Similarly, Masterson (1976; Masterson and Klein 1989), in an effort to demonstrate therapist trustworthiness and commitment, proposes an environment of 'communicative matching', an empathic 'refuelling' of the 'real self' (Masterson 1985). Here, attitudinal and behavioural neutrality are abandoned in favour of enthusiastic and supportive appreciation of patients' efforts in improving their lives.

Attachment therapists see lack of trust leading to a psychological state called 'insecure attachment'. They identify three types: 'avoidant', 'ambivalent' and 'disorganized'. The nature of patient insecure attachment indicates which parameter modifications need to be made. For instance, 'disorganized' patients, who tend to feel threatened by intimacy, may benefit from low-key support (Holmes 1992). 'Ambivalent' patients, who cling and are reticent to explore, need firm but reliable boundaries and a more active interpretative 'push'. 'Avoidant' patients, who fear rejection and may experience interpretation as intrusive, benefit from 'a more flexible and friendly therapeutic relationship' (Holmes 1993: 154). This matching of conditions to patient echoes Balint's (1986: 279) recommendation that the therapist 'be at the right distance . . . a distance that corresponds to the patient's actual need'.[8]

Subversion
Lacanians are dismissive of the alliance concept, since the ego (with which at least an essential aspect of the alliance is made) is deemed an 'imaginary' construct and 'the seat of illusions' (Lacan [1953–54] 1988: 62). It is imaginary in that it is formed when the baby (i.e. the 'subject') identifies with his or her 'specular *image*' (an ideal image

of wholeness seen in the 'mirror' of the mother's eyes). This ego-proffered experience of cohesion brings with it a sense of jubilant triumph but, because it contrasts so starkly with the subject's experience of a 'fragmented body' (Lacan [1955–56] 1993), it also brings a sense of precariousness, of alienation, of a 'gap' (Lacan [1953–54] 1988).

It is through the gaps in the 'imaginary order' which we weave, that **desire** – that continuous unconscious force that arises out of 'lack' and out of which, through our relationship with the perceived desires of others, we are constituted – reveals itself[9] (Lacan [1953] 1977, [1953–54] 1988, [1954–55] 1988, [1964] 1977). Since it is the task of therapy to enable patients to see the emerging truth about their desire, it might be thought that the id-alliance is more in keeping with the Lacanian approach. Yet this is not the case, certainly not at the start.

Lacanians suggest that patients come to therapy because of a crisis in their ego-oriented, imaginary worlds – a widening gap which threatens their stability. They come with a longing and a hope that the lack they feel may be assuaged, the gap filled. Since the source of desire *is* lack, there can be no id[10]/desire-alliance with those who would erase it and there can be no alliance with those who come not with a willingness to see the truth about their desire but a 'a will not to know' (Lacan [1955–56] 1993: 21). Indeed, patients come not with 'desire' but with 'demands': for a re-affirmation of their self-image, for the love in their *therapist's* eyes. Lacanians refuse to be drawn into this imaginary order of relating. Indeed, in an effort to uncover 'desire', rather than seeking to strengthen the patient's narcissistically oriented ego, they endeavour to unpick further the impostor's clothes: to reveal more acutely the frayed discontinuities, the tears, the gaps in patients' self-narratives which imaginary cohesion veils. In short, Lacanian therapists determine to frustrate patients' demands and engage them instead in a 'substitute satisfaction' – 'an endless dialectical process' (Lacan 1951: 12) or 'dialectic of desire' (Lacan [1960] 1977) which is the process of therapy itself. In the effort to create such engagement, it is not the patient's estranged desire that can be relied upon to provide the essential environmental condition for the therapeutic endeavour, but the therapist's.

The **desire of the analyst** (therapist) is 'analytically oriented', having been restructured by means of the therapist's own therapy: a desire to know, to search out ambiguity, to question everything, to attend to 'the Other' – that which is radically 'not-me'.[11] The therapist, spurning the discourse of the imaginary and with it his or her own ego-oriented role as person, adopts the purely functional role of attending to unconscious desire – the 'discourse of the Other'. It is an attentiveness that seeks to stimulate in patients an awareness of such discourse in themselves.[12]

For Lacanians, such stimulation best occurs not in an environment of rationalized 'safety', which is deemed simply to pander to the regressive illusion of cohesion and merger, but in one of subversive disruption. Epitomizing this disruptive environment is the **variable-length session** (Lacan [1953] 1977). For Lacanians, the analytic hour is an arbitrary invention quite out of tune with the timeless nature of the unconscious. Rather than encouraging surprise and spontaneity, two characteristics of the 'motion of desire', it promotes a stifling routine. Thus, by dismissing patients at any time – sometimes, though rarely, even after a few seconds – the therapist attempts to throw the ego off-guard, to underscore something significant which has been said or left unsaid and to ensure that moments of therapeutic import are not lost amidst the 'blah, blah, blah' of everyday talk.[13]

Recasting the analytic setting: a theatre for transference gathering

Emotional permeability
Kleinian therapists are also suspicious of the traditional notion of an alliance concept. For them, behind many a positive transference, a negative transference stalks. Indeed, whether positive or negative, all must be analysed. This is because transference is not seen just as a re-enactment of past relationships, but as a product of a 'here-and-now' way of relating called 'projection' (see Grant and Crawley, forthcoming).

Projection is a method of getting rid of aspects of ourselves, be they positive or negative, which we find difficult. In this way, we gain temporary relief but suffer long-term depletion. Like the world, the analytic setting – and in particular the therapist – becomes a depository for projections, a theatre for the patient's transference drama to be 'acted in' (Anna Freud, cited in Sandler *et al.* 1992). Thus, every utterance, every gesture is ripe for transference interpretation, offering insight into the patient's unconscious experience of the therapeutic relationship (Klein [1952] 1988). This is why Kleinians refer to the transference as the **total situation** (Joseph 1985).

The therapist's task in this transference-laden production is to help the patient re-introject (take in and digest) what has been projected (got rid of, spat out); to recognize that the dramatic parts cast, mirror aspects the patient is trying to disown. The therapist seeks to do this by encouraging the projected bits to coalesce in and around him in the transference, making them available for scrutiny and interpretation. This process, in which the therapist acts as tolerant stage manager to the patient's enacted script, is called **gathering the transference** (Meltzer 1968). The stage manager's role in this is non-directive. He must restrain himself from being 'co-actor in the scene which the patient re-enacts' (Heimann 1950: 83). He must refrain from all temptations to take directorial control.

Since all is transference, in Kleinian therapy, even more than in Classical Freudian therapy, there is no room for unscrutinized chit-chat, no such thing as simple physical contact or innocent social exchange. Timing is meticulously monitored. Extended sessions are prohibited and patient lateness or requests for time-changes offer material for interpretation. Reassurance is also shunned. If patient anxiety threatens the work, Kleinians interpret rather than reassure. 'Deep interpretation' offers understanding and thus safety (Rosenfeld [1987] 1990), while reassurance can communicate the therapist's difficulty in dealing with patient hostility, leaving the patient insecure.

Kleinian therapists feel but do not reveal what they feel. Self-disclosure obscures the transference and is susceptible to unhelpful patient interpretation, for example therapist as robber-mother, stealing space and time. Thus Kleinian therapists, even more than their Freudian counterparts, remain strictly anonymous. Indeed, so keen are they to do so, their consulting rooms tend to be spartan and their dress intentionally bland. All conditions are arranged for minimum external distraction and maximum focus on internal drama.

Although dramatic, this meticulously reserved stage management may sound cold, intellectual, even persecutory. It is often criticized as such (e.g. Balint [1968] 1989; Kernberg 1980). Yet to understand the patient's psychic script, therapists must do more than watch. They must 'enter the subjective world of the patient' (Hinshlewood 1991: 466). Paradoxically, they do this by allowing their patients' feeling states to enter into them.

It is through the counter-transference that Kleinian therapists get to know those aspects of their patients which have entered into them. Instead of remaining unfeeling and detached, they use their emotional response as 'an instrument of research' (Heimann 1950: 81).[14] Balance is crucial: subjective emotional engagement yet objective rational detachment; a 'willingness to contact the patient's anxieties' yet 'not . . . be overwhelmed by them' (Jaques 1982: 503); to permit 'invasion' yet 'resist capture' (Segal 1977). It is partly in an effort to 'resist capture' that other environmental conditions are so severe.

Containment

The ultimate aim of the Kleinian therapist's emotional engagement is to gain greater understanding. This understanding is used to make interpretations aimed at stimulating psychic change. Yet some neo-Kleinians suggest a therapeutic process is activated in the very condition of being with the patient in this counter-transferential way. The therapeutic potential of this condition is intimated in the concept of **containment**.

This term describes a process that forms part of healthy mother–infant relations (Bion [1959] 1984). The wordless infant, unable to deal with formless, seemingly overwhelming anxieties, projects them into mother. Mother, allowing these communications to penetrate, experiences their assault. If she can tolerate this, slowly meaning may emerge. On the basis of intuited meaning, she can then respond. In this way, the infant learns that anxiety can be thought about. It does not have to be expelled. Thus he re-introjects not only the anxiety, now modified by thought, but some aspect of the mother's capacity to think.

Like the mother, the therapist provides a containing role: a radically developed, three-dimensional, intuitively responsive, 'blank-screen'.[15] Tolerating the patient's projected anxieties, the therapist provides conditions that enable the patient to re-introject the projected parts of him or herself, to think. Since this unconscious process is collaborative, it has been referred to as the neo-Kleinian version of the alliance (Bollas 1990, cited in Sandler *et al.* 1992).

The therapeutic condition of mind required for this thoughtful permeability is **reverie** (Bion [1962] 1984). Reverie describes a calm receptivity in which the mind processes sense-oriented data. Form is given to formlessness, thought to the previously unthinkable and dreadful anxiety is 'named'. Reverie is a rich conceptual development of the condition of 'evenly suspended attention'.

Such mindfulness is not possible if therapists cling to information about their patients from past sessions, nor if they harbour hopes of what route the therapy might take. The emotional reality of the patient's experience can only be intuited in the moment of deep relaxation, where the therapist bears the state of **not knowing** and is **without memory or desire** (Bion [1967] 1988).[16] Thus, in hope of meaning – what Coltart (1986) refers to as 'faith' – the therapist employs a 'penetrating beam of darkness; a reciprocal of the searchlight', which more readily enables the 'light' of the patient's material to be seen (Bion [1974] 1990: 37, cited in Casement [1985] 1990).

The ability to bear not-knowing is called **negative capability** (Bion

[1970] 1984): the capacity to dwell 'in uncertainties, mysteries, doubts, without any irritable reaching after fact and reason' (p. 125).[17] This concept may be usefully related to that of **essential neutrality** (Franklin 1990): a willingness to maintain an 'open-ended' attitude towards every aspect of the therapeutic process so that no meaning is ever final and no 'truth' ever complete. Yet the capacity for essential neutrality – for sustaining a state of not-knowing – must be rooted in a 'reservoir of experience, thought and theoretical knowledge' (Coltart 1986: 5). Bion thus urges a dual perspective – knowing and not knowing, a type of **binocular vision**. Nonetheless, he stresses the importance of not imposing knowledge on the unfamiliar, simply as a way of relieving anxiety.

Congruent with a traditional Kleinian perspective then, neo-Kleinians act as receivers of patients' dramatic projections. They agree to subjective encounter. Yet they not only receive, but give something of their own back: something which is pre-verbal and non-interpretative. What they give is a condition of mind, a capacity for **bare attention**: for non-attached, non-judgemental awareness of what happens in us and to us from moment to moment. Here the language of psychodynamics meets the language of Buddhism (Coltart 1992, 1996; Epstein 1996). It is the introjected condition of meditative mindfulness that may offer hope of true psychic change.

The analytic setting revisited: a nursery for developmental redress

Holding
Post-war developmental theorists and researchers (e.g. Winnicott [1960a] 1990; Mahler 1968; Bowlby [1969] 1982; Kohut 1971; Stern 1985; Brazleton and Cramer 1991), which include therapists from the Object Relations and Self Psychology Schools, argue that psychological distress is not just a result of unresolved internal conflicts, but of real failures of real environments. Pointing out these failures, or interpreting behaviour as an outcome of them, has little therapeutic effect. What is needed is the affective processing of the original traumatizing experience, and the right environmental conditions in which this processing can occur. This is the purpose of the **corrective emotional experience** (Alexander and French 1946). Here the analytic setting adopts a new guise: a nursery for developmental redress.

Although most theorists tend to emphasize the difference between their approaches and the controversial 'corrective' concept (e.g.

Winnicott [1965a] 1990), there is a common perspective: the thera-peutic import of a **new beginning**. This means the patient regresses 'to a point before the faulty development started', not as a form of infantile retreat, but 'regression for the sake of progression' (Balint [1968] 1989: 132).[18]

Winnicott ([1954a] 1992) talks of a 'healing mechanism' inherent in regression: the patient's unconscious search for an environment in which natural developmental capacity is naturally restored.[19] The therapist's job is simple: to provide conditions for this 'self-healing' (Bowlby 1988). These conditions are a product not of deprivation but **adaptation**, and they require the therapist to embark upon 'a second attempt at parenting' (Lomas 1987: 69).

Winnicott's ([1960a] 1990) version of such adaptive provision is the **holding environment**. Although now widely used to refer to a form of therapeutic environment, Winnicott coined the term to refer to the environment produced by the mother's meticulous at-tention to her newborn child. Such attention is possible because of a temporary condition of mind called **primary maternal preoccu-pation** (Winnicott [1956] 1992). In this state, she is capable of deep **empathic attunement** (Stern 1985). So keen is this attunement, both infant and mother exist in seamless oneness (Winnicott [1960a] 1990). The infant is hungry and wondrously the breast appears. Merged with her baby, she plays the role of **supportive ego**, sustain-ing the baby's omnipotent illusion, an illusion necessary for this early phase of growth.

As primary maternal preoccupation wanes, the holding environ-ment loosens. Small environmental failures begin to occur. 'Small doses' of reality press in upon the infant's omnipotence and upon his 'continuity of being'. These interrupting pressures are called 'impingements' (Winnicott [1960a] 1990). In well-timed, 'small doses', they help the infant to gain a sense of separateness. If, however, impingements occur too early or are too intense, the infant's experi-ence is not of a loosening hold but of being 'dropped'. Defending against this 'drop', he 'reacts' by 'holding' himself. The formation of a 'False/Caretaker Self', behind which the 'True Self' hides, is just such a 'reactive' selfholding. This is a form of developmental arrest (Winnicott [1960b] 1990).

The unrelenting demands of the infant – his ruthless love (Winnicott [1954b] 1992) – provide good reason for a mother to 'drop' her baby: to impinge by asserting her own needs or by with-drawal. Yet if the infant is to develop healthily, the mother must 'survive' his ruthless love and, though hating him, hold on. The mother who manages, without traumatically impinging, to 'hate', survive and hold on, Winnicott calls **good-enough** and it is the garb of 'good-enough mother' that Winnicott urges the therapist to don.

Winnicott argues that with more disturbed patients – those in 'need of regression' – therapists may have to make radical modifications to the standard condition of non-gratification. They must, through deep empathic attunement characteristic of primary preoccupation, provide a holding environment for the patient which cannot be seen in terms of gratifying wishes but of meeting needs. And 'if the need is not met, the result is not anger, only a reproduction of the environmental failure situation which stopped the processes of self growth' (Winnicott [1954a] 1992: 288).

This holding imperative may lead to striking deviations in the management of the analytic setting, including the use of extended sessions, sitting alongside patients, serving coffee, and so on.[20] One particularly striking deviation involves the use of touch. Winnicott, critical of 'rigid analytic morality' regarding touch, suggests it might be the very contact the patient most requires. Balint and Bowlby echo this view; the latter seeing touch meeting a real attachment need. On occasions, then, Winnicott holds patients' hands (e.g. see Little 1990) and even describes rocking a woman's head. This is a very literal form of holding and of ego support in which, like mother and infant, therapist and patient 'merge'. Two famous papers (Pedder [1976] 1986; Casement [1982] 1986) argue the benefits and dangers of such adaptational extremes. In addition, 'token care' may be proffered in the form, for example, of giving patients small objects to which they have become attached to sustain them between therapy sessions, or by providing something simple to drink or eat during therapy, or a blanket to keep them warm. For most patients though, Winnicott suggests the standard analytic setting provides holding enough.

Although, generally, psychodynamic therapy views reassurance as unhelpful, Winnicott ([1954a] 1992: 292) suggests the 'whole set-up of psychoanalysis is one big reassurance' (see also Modell 1976). Each component of the setting emulates an aspect of the reassuring holding environment. For example, for the duration of the session and for a set number of sessions every week, the therapist is 'preoccupied' with the patient, a preoccupation which is at the service of the patient's 'continuity of being'. The therapist ensures the therapeutic space is safe from 'impingements', be they physical or in the form of his or her own 'moral judgement' or needs. The therapist remains emotionally available, evident in his or her 'positive interest' (love) and the 'strict start and finish' (hate). The therapist is not hurt by the patient's aggressive thoughts or fantasies or by the patient's 'ruthless love'. Neither crumbling nor withdrawing, the therapist 'survives' (Winnicott [1954a] 1992).

The therapist's **emotional availability**, even to the point of hating, is a long way from Freud's surgeon who 'puts aside all his feeling'. Yet the relentless assault of a regressed patient's ruthless love inevitably elicits just such a response. Indeed, the patient may seek it. Drawing on his experience of fostering a disturbed child, Winnicott ([1947] 1992: 199) comments that love is inadequate once the child, gaining hope, 'starts to test out the environment . . . to seek proof of his guardian's ability to hate objectively'. To hate 'objectively', the therapist must 'survive', must tolerate hating and still 'hold on'. Only then, when objective hate is perceived by the patient as proof that even the most unacceptable aspects of him are known, can he begin to believe in being loved (Phillips 1988).

Play

The mother/therapist's non-retaliatory survival allows the infant/patient to utilize natural aggression in the pursuit of **play**. The capacity to play is thus a developmental achievement and a precondition for standard, therapeutic work. If patients cannot play, the therapist's task is to ensure that they can (Winnicott [1971] 1974).

For play to occur, there needs to be a play area. This area is called a **transitional space** (Winnicott [1971] 1974). It is transitional because it bridges two other spaces: the omnipotently ruled, inner subjective space and the too often impotently inhabited, outer objective one. In the transitional space, the child plays with **transitional objects** such as bits of blanket. The essence of a good transitional object is that it belongs to the child – is almost an extension of him – yet is not him. He can love it, hate it, cuddle it, beat it, yet having no will of its own, it does not respond, except in a way that he imagines it responds. In effect, he can playfully externalize his thoughts, feelings and fantasies without incurring the real consequences of doing so.

The therapist can be viewed as being a type of transitional object for the patient. Playing with the therapist – investing him or her with thoughts, feelings, wishes – the patient imagines, discovers, grows.[21] To maintain the potential of this role, the therapist must not overly impinge. This is difficult, since interpretation is a type of impingement. Suddenly, the transitional object speaks! Thus Winnicott

([1971] 1974) recommends interpretative tentativeness. And, in any case, he warns, 'clever interpretations' can lead to patient False-Self compliance.

For Winnicott, 'playing' is more important than 'knowing' (Abram 1996). Although, like dreams and free associations, play provides a 'gateway to the unconscious' (Winnicott [1964] 1991), it is the activity itself, and not necessarily the interpretation of it, that promotes self-discovery, self-growth. Thus the environmental conditions of the transitional space, by allowing play, provide both milieu and method for the patient's 'creative', 'spontaneous' acts of True-Self discovery. These are moments of mutative 'surprise' (Winnicott [1971] 1974).

Narcissistic alliance or misalliance?
Environmental failure theory – and its accompanying adaptive conditions practice – has been widely criticized. The main concern is that this approach confirms the patient as passive victim and underplays the contribution of internal conflicts (Mitchell 1988). Furthermore, abstinence and neutrality are seen as being abandoned to counter-transference gratification. This can subvert the therapeutic work (Segal [1981] 1986). Underpinning these criticisms is the concept of 'primary narcissism' (Freud [1916–17] 1991). This suggests we want to return to a womb-like environment where immediate nutritional satisfaction allows no room for anxious dread. It follows that thera-pists need to refrain from fuelling developmentally regressive ten-dencies with the nurturing conditions inherent in the re-parenting model.

There is, however, plenty of material to suggest the notion of primary narcissism is 'absurd' (Lomas 1987). Fairbairn (1952), for example, describes an infant born not with the need to retreat, but to explore. Mother–infant studies (e.g. Bower 1977; Eigen 1980; Stern 1985; Brazleton and Cramer 1991) similarly all suggest a life which is vital, adventurous and quickly attuned to the external world. These challenges to the absolutism of primary narcissism offer some of the best evidence that environment matters. By inference, the conditions of the therapeutic environment may matter too: not just as a 'vehicle' of success, but as a therapeutic road to cure. It is ironic, then, that an approach which makes most mileage of nurturing conditions, is one whose theoretical base is a radical development of the principle of narcissism itself.

Kohut (1971) epitomizes those psychodynamic theorists who see psychological distress as being caused by developmental deficit. He proposes that this deficit results from parental failure to meet infant narcissistic needs, in particular **the need to be mirrored** and **the need to idealize**.

The mirroring need is met by parent delight and approval. In his parents' proud expressions, the infant perceives a 'grandiose self-object', an object which is not entirely distinguishable from himself but which could not come into being were it not for his parents' loving eyes. After sufficient mirroring, the grandiose self-object is internalized, imbibed like a reorganizing glue. This 'transmuting internalization' enables the infant's disorganized self to reorientate itself more cohesively around a sense of self-worth.

The idealizing need is met when the infant finds a parent whom it can cast as omniscient guardian. Whatever chaos ensues, the 'idealized parental imago' (another self-object) remains dependably calm. The illusion is: 'You are perfect; but then, I'm part of you' (Kohut 1971: 27). Again, gradually, transmuting internalization enables the infant self to reorientate, this time around a core of self-control and purposeful ideals.

Without the meeting of these needs, the self is left 'disorganized' rather than 'cohesive'. The disorganized self flounders in chaotic narcissistic immaturity. Unmirrored, it is forced to seek consolation in bursts of boastful grandiosity. Denied the opportunity to idealize, it is doomed to wander purposelessly, lacking in essential optimism or joy.

In the therapeutic environment, these deficits create a complex 'bipolar transference'. At one pole, the 'conflictual transference' enacts and defends against the patient's fears of further self-object failure. At the other pole, in the 'self-object transference', the patient longs for the therapist to meet his developmental needs. For Self Psychologists, while conflictual transference provides material for interpretation, self-object transference requires appreciative acceptance and a responsiveness that seeks to make sure these needs are understood and even met (Stolorow *et al.* 1987).[22] Thus the therapist must respond by maintaining an **oscillating bipolar neutrality** (Wolf 1983), one which provides the patient with the subjective experience both of **optimal frustration** and **optimal empathy** (Kohut 1984; Stolorow 1986).

Narcissistic needs are met by the parent/therapist who non-defensively makes himself **available for self-object usage** – for mirroring and idealizing. This availability is established in conditions of sustained **empathic resonance** (Kohut 1977), resulting from the therapist's empathic attunement. Only in these conditions can transmuting internalizations occur.

Empathy

Empathy is not a condition invented by Kohut. Fliess's (1942) term for it is 'trial identification', the therapist's capacity to split his ego and with one half step over the boundary between himself and the patient. This type of temporary regressive merger matches well Kohut's own definition (Elson 1987). Yet what is so significant about Kohut's contribution is not so much his definition as his use of it. Certainly he emphasizes the importance of 'prolonged empathic immersion' (Kohut 1971), of empathically experiencing the patient's world. Yet, more radically, he stresses the need for therapists to disclose the empathic understanding they have acquired. It is the non-judgemental communication of this understanding (Goodman 1992) that leads patients to realize that, contrary to their experiences in childhood, the sustaining echo of empathic resonance is indeed available in this world (Kohut 1984). Empathy thus becomes not only a necessary therapeutic condition in which affective alliance bonds are cemented and cognitive insights gleaned, but a method for renewing hope and, possibly, even for making developmental amends.

To what extent empathy alone is therapeutically sufficient is not clear, and different schools of Self-Psychology have given different degrees of prominence to this aspect of Kohut's work. Certainly, empathy may be seen as evidence of the therapist's containing function (Tansey and Burke 1985), a function which, like the holding environment, provides conditions for reactivating the 'original developmental tendency' (Kohut 1977). Yet, drawing on Kohut's later writings, some psychodynamic therapists go further. For them, the 'ambience of interested and attuned responsiveness' may gratify the needs of 'arrested aspects' of the patient's self by offering an experience of therapist as self-object (Wolf 1991: 128) – one which 'facilitates the resumption of developmental growth and the "repair" of self defects' (Eagle and Wolitzky 1997: 239). Abstinence, though not entirely dismissed, is heavily criticized and the key concept of optimal deprivation is replaced by **optimal provision** (Linden 1994).

In some ways, Kohut gave the cue for this. Recognizing the patient's 'enormous need', he advocates, at times, a 'reluctant compliance with the childhood wish' (Kohut in Elson 1987: 39). Not averse to demonstrating 'deep involvement' and 'concern', whether it be through 'warmth' of voice or words, he even relates an instance in which he offers a female patient his fingers to suck (Kohut 1981, cited in Clarkson 1995). In effect, interpretation is not what is on offer here since, to adapt Kohut's comments regarding good parenting, it is not so much what the therapist *does* that influences the patient as what the therapist *is* – empathic, available, reassuringly non-defensive, warm (Kohut and Wolf 1978).

Other Self Psychologists are clear about the therapeutic limits of empathic availability and reassuring warmth (Bacal and Newman 1990). Although the patient may need mirroring, they do not see it as the therapist's job actively to mirror. Rather, through 'tactful, nonhurtful, nonhumiliating' interpretation, the therapist appreci-ates the need and explains its psychic role (Goldberg 1978, 1988). This is to suggest that 'being understood is a maturing environment' (Friedman 1986) but not that 'understanding heals' (Levant and Shlien 1984, cited in Clarkson 1995). Certainly, the early Kohut (1971) sees the desire to 'cure *directly*' through empathy and 'the giving of loving understanding' as 'overbearing', 'annoying' and most probably evidence of 'the therapist's unresolved omnipotent fantasies' (p. 307).

Criticisms made of empathy's elevation from necessary condition to exclusive approach focus on its tendency to weaken objectivity. Its intuitive nature may lead to rationalizing errors of technique (Shapiro 1974), ignoring the therapist's own pathological projec-tions (Langs 1976) and neglecting the interpretation of conflict and defence (Kernberg 1980). For therapy to progress, the dynamic of empathic merger must be worked free of and a perspective of separate objectivity reaffirmed. Thus, although empathy promotes a stable, nurturing environment of 'mutual adaptation' (Schlesinger 1994), it also conspires to restrict growth (Winer 1994). In short, it may be necessary, but like love, it is not enough (Blum 1981).

Therapeutic failure
Winnicott and Kohut are sceptical of the therapeutic value of condi-tions of deliberate frustration. However, they do not argue that these conditions can be avoided or that they are not therapeutically valu-able. After all, without some degree of environmental failure, what opportunity is there for individuals to flex their developmental muscle?

Kohut (1984) refers to therapeutically valuable failures as **optimal failures**. For example, as long as children experience a foundation of sufficient mirroring, when a parental mirroring failure does occur, they have an opportunity to draw on the self-object mirror already internalized. This helps to consolidate the cohesive structures already in place. In therapy, it is the creative use of therapist empathic failure within a field of mostly sustained empathic resonance that pushes the therapy along (Chused and Raphling 1992).

For Winnicott ([1960a] 1990), the mother/therapist who does not at some point fail to meet her infant's needs, impinges as surely as if she had never held him. After all, in the space between a realization of a need and the gratification of it, 'the creative gesture, the cry, the protest' (p. 51) – the very stuff of communication – is generated. If there is no space, there is no creation. By analogy, the therapist must '*not* know the answers except in so far as the patient gives the clues' (p. 50). In an environment devoid of pre-emptive knowing, inevitable failures evoke inevitable anger. The therapist who survives such anger gets 'used' (Winnicott [1968] 1974).

Indeed, the patient may need to actually 'manoeuvre' therapist failures. Such manoeuvring is instigated by the patient's unconscious hope that he or she has found an environment in which old environmental failures can be experienced for the first time; or, to add paradox to paradox, where the patient can 'remember something that has not yet happened' (Winnicott 1974). It has not 'happened' because, at the time of the first failure, the self was not sufficiently organized to process the experience. Instead, it reacted defensively, prompting False Self organization. In the holding environment, the patient is given the opportunity to process affectively, to respond rather than react. Thus 'we succeed by failing – failing the patient's way' (Winnicott [1963] 1990: 258). This provides an ironic twist to the concept of 'cure by corrective experience'.

The last cluster of failures coalesces around the growing presence of therapist as real person.[23] This is particularly important at termination, but may also be crucial at times of therapeutic impasse. The therapist, bearing the 'reality principle' of his existence, can be likened to the mother who, re-emerging from maternal preoccupation, suddenly remembers herself and her own mind.

Further proof of the therapist's real and independent being comes from his 'deficiencies'. The admission of some of these may help patient and therapist 'let go of one another more easily when they have had enough' (Klauber 1986: 213). One such deficiency – universal rather than idiosyncratic – is the inevitable failure to totally understand (Winnicott [1963] 1990). Only if the therapist 'can free herself from special claims to knowledge in the relationship' can the patient claim ownership of the therapeutic work (Lomas 1987: 11). In turn, gradually accepting the therapist's shortcomings, the patient may come to renounce the wish to change her into 'cooperative partner' and turn instead towards a reality in which someone better suited for such a purpose might be found (Balint [1965] 1985).

Limiting the analytic setting: terminal conditions

Significantly, all psychodynamic practices have shifted towards briefer work of less frequency. Such a shift, prompted more by economic pressures than therapeutic efficacy, has led to a modification of certain therapeutic conditions. One of the most notable conditions stipulated is the patient's state of mind before therapy. They should have an awareness of underlying conflicts, an ability to trust and to disclose, a capacity to access a variety of affects, and a curiosity and willingness to engage in therapy despite discomfort. In effect, brief therapy demands they have a fair degree of psychological maturity, a lack of severity in terms of disturbance, a capacity to form a strong working alliance and a high degree of motivation.

A focus to the work is also key. Patient free association must be tempered by a capacity to select an area of 'conflicting wishes' (Sifneos 1987), while the therapist's attitude must shift from evenly suspended to **selective attention** and **neglect** (Malan 1976). Unable to 'wait for the material to bubble up' (Davanloo 1978, cited in Coren 1996: 31), brief therapy therapists thus take an **active approach**.[24] They challenge, provoke (Davanloo [1980] 1993), relentlessly pursue focal issues and, abandoning the position of blank screen, by behavioural or didactic means may actively disconfirm patients' views of them (Sifneos 1987). Although critics see such activity as authoritarian, even invasive (Moss 1985), others suggest open-ended therapy carries with it its own covert suggestiveness (Grünbaum 1984) and that brief therapy therapists are simply more explicit about their influence and role (Messer and Warren 1995).

The therapies alluded to above align themselves with the drive-discharge paradigm. More recently, relational-based brief therapies have arisen from research work (see Luborsky 1984; Strupp and Binder 1984; Weiss *et al.* 1986; Horowitz 1988). As with their open-ended counterparts, though not ignoring the import of insight, the role of a new, corrective experience is foregrounded. Thus, for example, the **helping alliance**, rooted as it is in Freud's ([1912b] 1958) 'unobjectionable positive transference', though still used to support the work of interpretation, is also seen as a primary source of therapeutic change (Luborsky 1984).

Ironically, though all these therapies – both drive-discharge and relational – are brief, none provide a theoretical rationale for their most radically modified condition: **time**. In contrast, Time Limited Psychotherapy (Mann 1973), as its namesake suggests, places time at its core.

Mann (1973) suggests time, for a child, is limitless. This perspective is rooted in the illusion of omnipotence, of fusion with the mother, of a world where pleasure-seeking prevails. Only later, as the reality of 'calendar' time encroaches, does painful disillusion set in.[25] This shift in time perspective captures the 'recurring life crisis' of separation-individuation and its attendant losses with which each person is constantly confronted. Thus Time Limited Psychotherapy, both in terms of what, through its therapeutic nature, it re-evokes (the long-ing for limitless understanding, for pleasure, for fusion) and what, through its condition of brevity, it provokes (the 'horror of time', 'the scythe', the *dead*-line), focuses on 'mastery of separation anxiety and failures to deal with it' (Messer and Warren 1995: 24).[26]

To bring these central conflicts to the fore, to manage them and to deal with them, a three-phase approach in which the therapist attends to promoting certain conditions is advocated. In the early phase, environmental conditions are informed by gratification. Mirroring, affirming, empathizing, supporting, holding; the ther-apist seeks to establish the alliance and play to the patient's magical expectations. Keeping the focus on the central issue, the regressive tendency, is also limited.

In the second phase, frustration is key. Sharpening the focus, the therapist refuses patient overtures of merger. Only once these dual conflicting conditions are alive in the therapy are transference dynamics, in the final phase, addressed. The focus then is on reac-tions to termination, and the therapist, playing a suggestive, educative role, supports the patient in renegotiating the experience of loss. In this way, Time Limited Psychotherapy offers both comprehensive method and satisfying rationale for the brief approach. However, whether all psychological disturbance can be encapsulated within a single theme, remains a matter of debate (see Grand *et al.* 1985).

Conclusion

The concepts outlined in this chapter have been generated by differ-ent psychodynamic schools. Nonetheless, no school is an island and no therapist is immune to the beliefs and practices of orientations outside his or her chosen theoretical sphere. Although, according to whatever doctrinal exhortation, some therapists strive towards sustaining conditions of frustration while others aim for a more gratification-oriented approach, in the reality of the therapeutic en-counter, it is the dyad's grappling with the dynamic tension between these conditions which characterizes the environment and fuels much of the clinical work. This uneasy grappling forces therapists into minor acts of non-doctrinal spontaneity. These acts may leave therapists guilt-ridden, concerned that the way they have behaved isn't 'kosher'. Yet 'any therapist worth his salt', both consciously and unconsciously, modifies his behaviour to suit 'specific patients on the basis of his interaction with those patients' (Sandler 1983: 38).[27]

The therapeutic ground of 'core conditions' is well delineated and well trod. Yet, as each individual therapist steps tentatively into the consulting room to meet with each individual patient, he or she engages in both a unique encounter demanding unique conditions and an endless, age-old debate – about the effects of nature and nurture, about the importance of individuality and relatedness, about the therapeutic value of discipline and love.

RESPONSE AND REFLECTION

RICHARD HAZLER

N.B. has provided a thoughtful, detailed, analytic look at the core conditions of a psychodynamic orientation. With no need to extend on the wealth of information provided, the opportunity presents itself to very briefly focus attention on a still evolving struggle which N.B. touches upon within the psychodynamic field: the condition of therapist as a role versus a person in the therapeutic relationship.

Freud's original conservative approach to clients was one based on the dangers of a therapist 'letting oneself go'. The same internal pressures that were the heart of client problems were also recognized to be working within therapists and therefore had to be kept under tight control. The therapist was to provide a therapist role rather than a full person in order to establish the necessary relationship conditions for therapy. The most efficient way to ensure such control and provide the appropriate conditions was to keep the human being of the therapist out of the session and the objective and technically correct therapist fully in charge, or, as N.B. has put it, one who, 'like a surgeon, scrubs himself clean'. In Freud's case, this meant the therapist would be visually out of sight, physically out of touch, emotionally out of reach and, related to personal information, strictly a receiver and objective interpreter.

Many later psychodynamic therapists recognized the problems associated with, and even the impossibility of, eliminating the person of the therapist from sessions (Langs 1978; Gill 1988; Peters 1991). Others went even further by taking positions in favour of using more direct human intervention by the therapist to maximize relationship conditions (Ehrenberg 1984, 1992; Stolorow *et al*. 1994; Trop and Stolorow 1997). The struggle has become one of how much to fear the internal dimensions of therapists, how much to allow two human beings to come into personal yet therapeutic contact, and the ways in which these two directions can best be managed.

Phrases like 'contamination of the therapist', 'purge the personality of the therapist', 'fear of counter-transference' and others highlight the extreme distrust psychoanalysts have of therapists allowing the full person inside the therapeutic setting. When they do advocate much greater emphasis on human involvement, such as Ferenczi's ([1932] 1980) mutual analysis, it is only considered in the context of 'last resort' (Dupont 1988). Less controversial approaches give attention to the therapist as a more personalized partner (Zetzel [1958] 1987) who can display direct affective engagement in a more egalitarian relationship (Ehrenberg 1984).

Clearly, there has been movement in the psychodynamic field away from Freud's extreme model of fully objective relationship conditions to a recognition that nothing can keep all therapist personality variables out of the relationship (Jacobs 1991; Peters 1991). The practical trend has become not one of simple elimination of therapist personality from therapy, but instead how to recognize, control and utilize it as a core condition for facilitating therapy. It is a movement towards an optimal relationship condition between therapists and clients that gives clients more credit for their capacity to handle themselves and their interactions with the therapist; a relationship condition where therapists have freedom to recognize that they have more to offer from their internal reactions and where they are not tied to strict objectivity. It is an evolution towards conditions of more freedom for therapist and client to be who they are in sessions rather than only the roles they are expected to play.

Although the evolution towards more human openness as a relationship condition of psychodynamic therapy seems clear, it is also constrained by other core beliefs. Freud's original distrust of therapists' ability to productively control their own inner turmoil remains a key factor in setting the facilitative relationship conditions of psychodynamic therapy. All movement towards more open interaction between therapist and client continues to be weighed against this distrust and the associated therapeutic relationship dangers involved. The result is that psychodynamic therapists will continue to fall more on the 'therapist as role' side of the relationship-conditions continuum even as they move, over time, and with conservative hesitation, towards the 'therapist as a person' end.

CHAPTER 3

Core conditions of the cognitive-behavioural environment

RICHARD HAZLER

Introduction: a collision of internal and external variables

'Please help me with my dad. I don't know what to do next and you are my last hope.' The call was from Tina, a middle-aged woman who was frantic about her father's condition.

'Charles, that's my dad, hasn't left the house in months, not even to go to the post for the mail. I have to bring that in for him along with everything else. He doesn't eat, won't go out to get food, has unplugged the phone and even accuses me of sneaking around the house to steal things. He gets worse every day and I just can't keep this up. You helped me before in therapy. Please help him now . . . But I have to warn you, he'll not leave the house and thinks therapists are witch doctors. He thinks you just tricked me out of my money and blames you for my eventual divorce. There is probably no reason you would want to work with him, but I have hope that you can help. Will you please do it for me?'

Charles is clearly in need of therapy, as his behaviours are counter-productive to effective living. But everything about the therapy situation would be difficult. He is not asking for help, does not want therapy and does not believe in therapists, while his very refusal to leave the house reduces the ability of the therapist to control the therapeutic environment.

Based on his daughter's frantic assessment, it would appear that Charles' physical stamina, cognitive functioning, emotional stability and social network are all in disarray. There are plenty of places to look for interesting information about the environmental etiology of Charles' problems and about his irrational thoughts. A diagnosis could be built on such information. Strategies could be implemented to change the irrational thoughts and modify behaviours in more productive directions. But knowing what information to acquire and how to implement effective cognitive-behavioural strategies is not enough. The crucial first problem for the therapist is one of creating the necessary foundation to build upon. That foundation is an environment which facilitates information collection and corrective therapeutic techniques.

The facilitative aspects of the therapeutic environment are not a favourite topic of cognitive-behaviourists. The cognitive-behavioural literature gives detailed attention to specific therapeutic techniques for specific problems. It does a thorough job of providing a scientific rationale for why these techniques work. Yet this thoroughness and attention to detail is not reflected in descriptions of how to prepare and manage the physical, emotional and interpersonal aspects of a facilitative cognitive-behavioural environment.

A brief review of the evolution of the cognitive-behavioural therapeutic environment will help clarify how the two diverse concepts of cognition and behaviour came to be connected. In turn, the history and current nature of this connection should help clarify how the design of cognitive-behavioural therapy's facilitative environment took on its present form.

Paradigms and perspectives

Before 1929, virtually all textbooks referred to psychology as a 'science of the mind'. This essentially cognitive perspective dominated the field at this time. It was a dominant position soon to be usurped.

Behaviourism became a major force in psychology early in the twentieth century. The fact that, between 1930 and 1970, over half the textbooks in print described psychology as a 'science of behaviour' serves to highlight its dynamic rise. Only in the 1980s did terms like 'mind' and 'cognition' begin to find their way back into standard textbook titles in significant numbers (Craighead *et al.* 1994). This twentieth-century textbook title trend reflects the evolution of psychotherapeutic theory, procedures, techniques and relationships.

Scientific experimentation on behaviours within highly **controlled environments** marked the behavioural beginnings of the CBT movement. This early stage saw cognitions frowned upon as irrelevant and only behaviours were considered valid for study. The experiments of Pavlov (1927) and Watson (Watson and Reyner, 1920), which drove the model of behaviourism for years, demanded that every effort be made to sanitize the experimental environment surrounding subjects so that only specifically selected variables could be applied, observed and tested for their influence. Things like interactions between the experimenter and subject were kept to an absolute minimum, as were any other variables thought to be extraneous.

Pavlov demonstrated how **classical conditioning** worked by isolating reflexes in dogs. A brash scientist named John Watson withheld naturally protective interpersonal variables from an 11-month-old child named Little Albert and, by adding new variables, trained the young boy to fear a white rat. Thus behaviourists learnt how to control animals and people by understanding and manipulating the environment around them. The facilitative environment needed for this to work was one in which order was fully maintained and the conditions were completely controlled by the researcher.

Skinner's (1938, 1953) **operant conditioning** allowed more freedom for things to happen on their own within the subject's environment, but the experimenter still maintained tight scientific control of the conditions and of the reinforcements to be added. Children were the easiest humans to control and therefore got most of the attention. Even Skinner's daughter was raised to a large degree in a form of Skinner Box (Skinner 1976). Little wonder that behaviourists acquired a reputation for providing a cold scientific environment that paid little attention to the dynamics of human interaction. Although the validity of this reputation has diminished over the years, the reputation itself has not.

Behaviourists succeeded in explaining much about human behaviour, but their own research revealed that what could not be explained was even greater. Results simply did not account for all the complex human variables that were related to human development and therapeutic change. Albert Bandura's (1965, 1971) reports of vicarious learning highlighted the shortcomings in the behaviourist understanding of what facilitates therapeutic change, making it clear that there was more that needed attention than simple stimulus–response behaviours.

Bandura's (1969, 1977) **social learning** theory gave greater emphasis to the importance of interpersonal interactions and the role of thinking in behaviours. Demonstrating that people could and would learn by simply watching others led therapists to model words and actions for their clients. A major evolutionary step thus emerged that changed therapists from simple designers and manipulators of controlled experiences, to active participants in relationship-experiments *with* clients.

Concepts derived from social learning theory helped fuel the cognitive revolution (Dember 1974) of the 1960s and 1970s. Leading this revolution, Aaron Beck (1979) and Albert Ellis (1962) devoted much attention to people's thought-processes, to their irrational assumptions and to methods for restructuring distorted patterns of thinking. Thinking was now assigned a primary role in determining why people felt and behaved the way they did, how they changed and what kind of therapeutic environment was necessary to facilitate such change.

The effect of the cognitive paradigm on the behavioural perspective was to create a therapy with a broader picture of clients and of how therapists need to interact with them. Gone is the notion of the therapist/researcher being external to the experiment. Modelling and teaching about thoughts, words, environment and action-taking now become key parts of the facilitative environment. Nonetheless, at the same time, the cognitive-behavioural environment hangs on tightly to its highly structured scientific methodology, characteristic of its behavioural roots. Orderly procedures, specific data collection and controlled experimentation continue to be core conditions both in the design and implementation of the facilitative therapeutic environment.

Core conditions

How does a therapist begin to tap into Charles' thinking when he will not come to the office and does not want to communicate? What environmental interventions and reinforcements can be instituted when Charles is in control of his limited environment or when Kristin, discussed in Chapter 1, has seized control of her therapist's office? What are the conditions that must be created to utilize cognitive-behavioural therapeutic techniques most effectively?

Order
Both cognitive and behavioural approaches to helping place tremendous importance on the belief that logic and reason point the way to understanding and directing one's life. It is a philosophical point of view that emphasizes rational, structured planning. No

wonder that such an organized view of people's lives carries over into highly **ordered therapy sessions**.

Reaching agreement on topics and setting a feasible agenda is a major priority for cognitive-behavioural therapists (Wright and Beck 1994). They want to be sure that the **agreed-to-agenda** has several key characteristics:

1 Items on the agenda are highly relevant to the client and sufficiently concrete for establishing directed actions.
2 The agenda can be accomplished in the session.
3 Time will be available to support past efforts by **following up** on material and assignments from previous sessions.
4 The session provides opportunities for developing new **homework assignments**.

These characteristics provide a visible model of the **logical process** of therapy, a model that the therapist uses to demonstrate consistency and effectiveness within the therapy session. Since this is the same rational, behavioural model that clients are asked to implement in their own lives, the process of therapy itself provides for both learning and practice of the model.

Charles and Kristin bring two different examples of how this order becomes a problem. Charles will not come in for therapy and does not want to meet with the therapist. Unless a therapist can find another way to begin to create some form of order in the relationship, there will not be the potential for demonstrating how the model works. Kristin, on the other hand, has come into the therapist's office. However, at least initially, she has set down her own model for how the sessions are to be run. In her case, the challenge to the cognitive-behavioural therapist will be to seek an order to the session that more closely fits the facilitative structure demanded for change to occur and continue over time. It is more likely that therapy will fail if the therapist allows Kristin to undermine the appropriate order of the session. The presence of an agreed-upon and reasonable therapeutic order for sessions helps therapists manage time efficiently, keep the session on task, coordinate homework and therapy efforts and assure continuity across sessions. These are all things that clients will need as they try to pull together the disassembled pieces of their lives. Additional immediate benefits for clients are that feelings of hopelessness and inadequacy are counteracted by breaking down seemingly insurmountable, complex problems and processes into manageable chunks (Wright and Beck 1994).

Data

To tackle the smaller constituent parts of the whole problem, a major emphasis on acquiring as much critical, detailed information as possible is required. This need for detailed information is a reflection of the continuing influence of cognitive-behavioural theory's experimental roots.

Historically, behavioural assessment began by seeking only directly **observable data**. Although such data continue to have major importance in cognitive-behavioural assessments, the individual's **cognitive processes** – beliefs, expectations, self-statements, imagery and attributions – now also play a vital role (Galassi and Perot 1992).

Without the ability to collect specific kinds of data on their clients, cognitive-behavioural therapists would be in a similar position to Pavlov having a dog, but no way to recognize consistency in how the dog acted before, during or after the classical conditioning experiment. It is essential, therefore, that therapists immediately begin seeking all possible relevant information from their clients as the individualization of therapy depends on this **data collection**.

The case of Kristin provides a more direct approach to data collection than does the case of Charles. Kristin has offered herself for limited observation and discussion of her experiences, so no matter what other difficulties she presents, first-hand data on her *are* available. Charles, on the other hand, is, as yet, not available, so the best source of data in his case is his daughter. This indirect source demands immediate use while, in the future, the best information can only come from direct contact with Charles and his immediate environment.

Motivation and availability

An orderly system of therapy and all the available data in the world will not help the therapist if the client is not motivated in at least two ways: first, to actively seek a more effective life-situation and, second, to be regularly involved in therapy (Kanfer 1996). In short, cognitive-behavioural therapists must have access to clients who want a different way of living. The problem is how to recognize and promote these critical conditions of **motivation** when they are not already available at desired levels.

Charles has hidden himself away in the house and does not wish to come out. We could make a guess at the fears, the irrational thoughts and, perhaps, even some past and present events that are promoting these apparently unproductive behaviours. But we must also understand that each of these factors serves a purpose for Charles.

If they add up to a situation in which Charles desires continuity more than change in his current life, then it will be difficult if not impossible to provide effective therapy. It may even border on unethical therapist behaviour to push Charles towards a different life-situation when he is not motivated to change. Therapy is meant to help clients acquire something closer to their personal view of a quality life and not to help therapists enforce their own picture of a 'good life' upon their clients.

The second aspect of motivation – the willingness to be involved in therapy regularly – clearly requires **client availability**. If Charles cannot be induced to begin and continue in a therapeutic situation, what hope is there for the therapist to create orderly and directed change. Obviously, the cognitive element of therapy requires intellectual contact, while access to behavioural aspects of the client's life is critical for behavioural evaluation and practice. Not surprisingly, without client availability, nothing therapeutic can be achieved.

There continues to be no well-accepted, comprehensive cognitive-behavioural definition of the term 'motivation'. Some cognitive-behavioural therapists continue to see motivation as an internal client factor. Were this the total picture, therapists would be at the mercy of people's motivation rather than being the *movers* of people and motivation. However, the interaction that is clearly necessary in therapy together with the need to promote client motivation makes the concept one that can best be viewed as an interpersonal interaction factor in the therapy process. It is the ability of therapists to increase and maintain client motivation while thoughts, behaviours and situations change that determines the degree to which an effective therapeutic relationship is realized.

Goals
Client motivation to change is closely connected to the need for specific **goal-setting** – another condition necessary for the effective practice of cognitive-behavioural therapy. What are the desired outcomes? What can be done to get there? How will we know when and if we have arrived at the desired outcome? These questions are critical because cognitive-behavioural techniques are more directive than most and, without specific, agreed upon goals to work towards, this **directive approach** would be analogous to asking a disoriented person in a dark room to take ten steps in ten different and 'correct' directions. Whether in a dark room or a therapy session, people must know where they are headed if they are to successfully find and follow the best route.

Both behavioural and cognitive strands of cognitive-behavioural therapy emphasize the role of specific goals, although the goals they emphasize are different in nature. **Behavioural goals** are situation-specific and results are expected to be clearly observable in the client's interaction with the environment (Morris and Morris 1992). **Cognitive goals** relate to excesses or deficits in thought-processes that can be seen in mental manipulation of ideas and emotions, but are less visible behaviourally (Kalodner 1995). By combining cognitive and behavioural perspectives, cognitive-behavioural therapy offers a more inclusive approach.

Therapy goals change regularly as environmental situations, therapist understanding and client thoughts and behaviours change. Initial goals for people like Charles or Kristin may be used as a way of evaluating whether therapy is even possible and, if it is, under what conditions. Only if the evaluation is positive will therapist and client move on to establish a **follow-up set of goals**. Such goals are more cooperatively reached with an emphasis on motivation and desires of the client.

Goals point therapists and clients in the logically chosen directions required by the directive and rational approach characteristic of cognitive-behavioural therapy. The directions suggested by goals are likely to be less than perfect and frequently in conflict with other goals. These apparent weaknesses in goal-setting are really a part of a decision-making process in which clients must test goals and ideas rather than accept them as 'right'. These conflicting ideas encourage a **hypothetical mindset** in clients, which is characterized by a constant testing and assessment of the accuracy of any given hypothesis.

Hypothetical mindset
Cognitive-behavioural therapists use client data and goals not so much to develop answers for clients, but to create new **hypotheses for testing** (Wright and Beck 1994). These hypotheses are predictions about what should occur if the analysis of the data is correct. The experimental culture of constantly using the flow of new data to create new hypotheses, which are then tested either in or outside the therapy sessions, is a core condition of cognitive-behavioural therapy.

Each time something is learned and placed in context with other information, it creates a new conceptualization of what and how an individual is influencing and being influenced by thoughts and environment. Utilizing these continuing changes is vitally important for human development, while absolute acceptance of any new conceptualization serves to halt the learning process in that area. Such aborted learning turns cognitive understandings into rigid biases and prejudices, and behavioural functioning becomes compulsive and inflexible. To be effective, new data must continually be sought, integrated with other information, and new expectations in the form of hypotheses prepared for later experimental testing.

The presence of this hypothetical mindset is manifest in the therapist's and the client's acceptance of the idea that no perceived knowledge is necessarily permanent. Conclusions are always being revised and consideration of how each new conclusion might impact upon therapy or upon clients' lives is a major part of all thinking and discussion. To some extent, most hypotheses will be proven wrong, but that is not failure. Rather, it is an expected part of the learning process where each failed hypothesis increases the information available to make the next one more accurate.

Kristin's doubts about the value of therapy for her are expressions of hypotheses she has developed from previous therapeutic experiences. Productive therapy should lead her to reject these hypotheses if the therapist can create better conditions and experimental designs than Kristin's previous therapists. The secret will be to help Kristin recognize the hypotheses under which she operates so that new data acquired in therapy can be seen as a valid reason to change her hypotheses and then to test new ones.

Charles has created a set of rigid thoughts and obsessive behaviours that will make the development of new hypotheses difficult. He is acting on what he considers 'unalterable facts' about himself and his environment. Only when therapy can proceed under the condition that *facts are only hypotheses to be tested*, will Charles be in a position to incorporate new information in such a way as to elicit productive changes.

Experimentation
Hypotheses only serve a practical function when they are tested for their accuracy in reality. Imagine that a therapist told Charles, 'Your fears are not real so you can stop worrying', or told Kristin, 'Change your behaviours and you will get more from therapy'. As correct as these statements might be, they will only gain factual status for clients and therapists and have therapeutic impact when they are tested to see if they have validity in reality. Thus the environmental conditions which facilitate cognitive-behavioural therapy are synonymous with those of an **experimental culture**. It is this culture which both promotes and is promoted by the designing and carrying out of

experiments, and it is these experiments which test the cognitive and behavioural validity of hypotheses (Wright and Beck 1994). **Cognitive experiments** test client thoughts along a logical–illogical continuum. Therapists use concepts and analogies to help clients discover whether a thought or belief can hold up to various tests of logic using available data. Each experiment is designed to reveal the strengths and flaws in cognitive processes so that, where necessary, these processes can be revised along more rational lines. **Behavioural experiments** focus on the actions and inactions of clients. Will actions follow words? How close to the hypothesized action was the implementation? What was the resulting effect of the action? Observation, classification and quantification of experimental results are necessary to develop effectively future hypotheses for testing.

Combining cognitive with behavioural experiments creates a more holistic perspective. Seeing how well verbal goals match behavioural actions highlights the consistencies and inconsistencies experienced by clients. An environment that encourages experiments and the learning that comes from them is essential to move on to therapeutic action-steps. Without acceptance of an experimental environment, there can be no next steps, since the supportable rationale needed to decide which hypotheses to reject and which outcomes to strengthen through reinforcement would be missing.

Environmental reinforcement
Environmental reinforcement is a condition that serves to strengthen, maintain or support desired behaviours and cognitions. The logical reasoning of cognitive-behaviourists is that, in the absence of reinforcing physical, mental, social or emotional conditions, the individual is provided with no reason to think or act in the same way twice. Therapists who want positive thoughts and actions to continue and negative ones to change or become extinct, must ensure the presence of conditions that reinforce desired outcomes.

One meaning of the term reinforcement is as a highly behaviour-specific technique or action applied to a client (Miller 1980). For example, a child is given a gold star, a horse gets a sugar cube, or a person is offered a compliment on their actions. This use of the word 'reinforcement' does not describe the core condition of reinforcement, but instead the technique or action used to create the condition.

Environmental reinforcement conditions can be any that allow some form of reward to be available to the client for appropriate thoughts or actions. Bandura's (1971) concept of **expectancy**

reinforcement, however, helped broaden this definition to include client cognitive expectations as reinforcing. That is to say, the animal or person might take some action with the expectation of being reinforced. Conditions can thus be created where simply the ability to provide a horse with a sugar cube when the appropriate action is accomplished becomes the means of reinforcing condition rather than the implementation of any individual reinforcement technique. Conversely, regular forgetting to bring the sugar cubes to the barn would reduce or eliminate that particular reinforcing condition.

The core condition of environmental reinforcements, therefore, is more than a matter of providing individual reinforcements in the form of treats, praise or relief from noxious elements. A facilitative environment is one in which the reinforcers are available, recognized and utilized. If these conditions were not available, the behavioural focus of cognitive-behavioural therapy would conclude that no new thoughts and behaviours could be maintained. There must be something valued by the client that comes from new thoughts and behaviours or there will be no reason to continue them.

Collaboration
Beck (1979) coined the term **collaborative empiricism** to describe the relationship between cognitive therapist and client. This description continued to fit as cognitive and behavioural therapies combined forces. Thus, in cognitive-behavioural therapy, through a series of experiments, client and therapist work *together* to test the validity of various hypotheses about the client's self and environment. The collaborative nature of the relationship that characterizes this way of working is not designed to be the actual healing mechanism, but instead serves to set the necessary conditions for therapy.

Horvath and Greenberg (1994: 135) use the analogy of anaesthesia's value to a medical operation to explain the role of the **collaborative relationship** in cognitive-behavioural therapy. Before the actual operation on an ailing organ can begin, anaesthesia is crucial. Much time and care must be taken with concocting the right mix of chemicals to ensure the correct environment. Once the anaesthesia is in effect, the surgery on the problem organ takes primacy. It is the surgery not the anaesthetic that has the reparative function. In a similar way, the collaborative dynamics of the therapeutic relationship provide the conditions where techniques can be used effectively, although the collaboration is not the corrective therapy itself.

The collaborative approach runs throughout therapy, but the dynamics change at different stages (Wright and Beck 1994). In the early stages, the therapist tends to act more as a teacher who, being active and directive, instructs clients in the experimental process and demonstrates how to use it to their benefit. Then, as clients learn to understand and utilize this process, they are given greater responsibility for the design and execution of experiments. The evolution of such a successful collaboration would see a client like Kristin increasingly recognize how her thoughts are connected to behaviours and how these behaviours bring negative costs along with some benefits. She would become more and more able to challenge those thoughts and behaviours through experimentation, which, most of the time, she would carry out for herself. In effect, the more controlling, active, teaching role played by the therapist early in the process becomes increasingly consultative in nature as clients take more responsibility for their own problem-solving (Wilson and Evans 1977). Clients who begin as passive, student-responders turn into directors and decision-makers. These evolving changes in the collaboration model produce a consistent and logical pattern, but variations within the client–therapist relationship create differences in the timing, nature and eventual effectiveness of this collaboration.

Relationship
The interpersonal dynamics between therapist and client were originally seen as being insignificant by early behaviourists. However, over the years, there has been growing recognition of the importance of the **therapeutic relationship** dynamics and the merging with cognitive therapy has strengthened that recognition. Increasing recognition, though, has never led to these variables attracting the same aggressive cognitive-behavioural scrutiny as logical confrontation and behavioural techniques. There is still comparatively little written in journals or textbooks about the therapeutic relationship and it is more often treated as the **non-specific variables** of cognitive-behavioural therapy (Raue and Goldfried 1994).

Ellis's (1962) early position on these issues was very similar to that of the behaviourists. He felt that things like **empathy** had little, if any, value in comparison to the more technical aspects of therapy. His mind seems to have changed little, but many others have. Most cognitive-behaviourists currently recognize that **warmth, genuineness** and accurate empathy are necessary in the therapeutic relationship to ensure the efficacy of cognitive-behavioural techniques (Beck *et al.* 1993). Burns and Auerbach (1996) practically combine the two positions, depicting how therapists must switch back and forth between placing emphasis on technique and giving relationship factors more attention as situational needs change.

Cognitive-behavioural research is limited on these non-specific variables, but there is support for their importance. Therapeutic empathy and warmth have been found to be correlated with the degree of in-session, client improvement (Persons and Burns 1985). In another study, the therapist variables of structuring and relationship-enhancement accounted for 60 per cent of the outcome differences, which was significantly more than could be accounted for by either variable alone (Alexander *et al.* 1976). More recent studies have demonstrated quite clearly that therapeutic empathy does have a significant effect on the therapeutic value of cognitive-behavioural therapy (Burns and Auerbach 1996).

Modern cognitive-behavioural therapists recognize that relationship development is a part of all their sessions and that, in working with clients like Kristin and Charles, direct attention to the relationship is especially important. Trust is obviously lacking for both these clients and anxiety is high. Consequently, it is the **relationship enhancement variables** that need focusing on early if a stage for the effective utilization of the most appropriate cognitive-behavioural techniques is to be created.

Applications

Cognitive-behaviourists spend most of their therapeutic thinking and acting-time on the cognitions and behaviours exhibited by clients. Strengths and weaknesses in client logic, action and environment are the most sought out pieces of information and the focus of therapeutic techniques. Textbooks produce volumes on what techniques to use, how to use them and why they need to be used. Journals are filled with practical applications and research related to which techniques work best and the most recent adaptations of them. What gets minimal attention in print are the conditions that need to be in place to enable cognitive-behavioural therapeutic techniques to be successful.

The literature seems to presume that cognitive-behavioural therapists automatically know what the best facilitative therapeutic environment includes and how to implement it. Therapist discussions around the coffee machine or water cooler tend to tell a different story. This is where discussions take place about struggles with technique implementation, unsatisfactory outcomes, personal reactions to clients, unmanageable resistance and a searching for anything that would allow them to use their best techniques more effectively. These are discussions about core facilitative conditions and how to apply them in practice.

Maintaining order

The examples of Charles not wanting to be in therapy and Kristin attempting to take control of the therapy process throw monkey wrenches into the therapist's bag of tricks. Cognitive-behavioural techniques need order in the environment if the well-planned activities are to have the calculated results. It will be the therapist's task to create and maintain the orderly situation necessary for the facilitation of the logical process of therapy.

The first task in the case of Charles will be to create an environment where he can be connected to therapy. Enlisting the daughter to get Charles into the counselling office would be an excellent start. The therapist would then be able to control the therapeutic environment while the simple step of leaving home and testing a less safe environment would produce cognitive and behavioural movement that could immediately become a focus of therapy techniques.

The therapist might also go to Charles' home if permission to do so was acquired and other options did not seem available. This contact would be less satisfactory, since it reduces therapist control of the environment. On the other hand, it could provide more comfort for the client and would allow the therapist to begin using some direct techniques that would be impossible if they did not get together at all. A last resort might be to teach the daughter some techniques for creating an environment with her father that would be better suited to cognitive-behavioural learning.

Kristin has come to the therapist, taken some physical control and questioned the potential of the therapist. In this case, the cognitive-behavioural therapist could worry less about Kristin's particular actions and do some structuring around agenda-setting, time constraints and homework activities. Laying out the process and showing confidence in its ability to work would be the general way of **creating initial order** for the client. Kristin could then be encouraged to make decisions about accepting to test the process and committing to involve herself further.

No-one could be sure how much Kristin or Charles would benefit from therapy, but with some order injected into the relationships, the opportunity to move forward with this rational, empirical therapy would be improved. Without creating and maintaining some form of order, there would be no potential to move forward in understanding and in taking actions that might help these two people.

Eliciting data
Kristin's in-session behaviour is immediately recognizable as a product of unhelpful previous learning. The simple recognition of the reason for Kristin's behaviour is a solid start to the collection of data on the client. What the therapist must not do is to over-utilize this limited initial data by drawing conclusions too early. Eliciting much more data will be critical throughout the process of identifying goals, designing experiments and evaluating results in a cyclical fashion.

Observations provide much of the clearest data for therapists, but those data need confirmation from the cognitions that are attached to clients' – in this instance, Kristin's – behaviours. The here-and-now nature of the behaviours provides timely access to the thoughts that may be directing her unusual words and actions. This immediate availability offers extremely valuable data that can be compared directly to Kristin's thoughts. For example, do her actions match her words or do her experiences match the expressions on her face? If she was talking about past or future events, these same comparisons would be much harder to make because the therapist could only see them through Kristin's selective memory and her choices of what to share.

Observation and discussion are the two key data sets in the development of a facilitative environment. They are the data sets that most closely reflect what is happening in therapy sessions and, therefore, allow the greatest opportunities to quickly adjust both the environment and techniques to best suit specific client circumstances. Other forms of data, including those derived from testing, client history and observations from friends and relatives, play an important part in overall therapy, but have less direct impact on the immediate maintenance of a therapeutic environment.

Tapping motivation
Kristin has come to therapy because she wants something more out of her life. She is also demanding more out of therapy than she has received previously. Her approach is to be controlling and demanding while placing responsibility on the therapist. This makes for a very uncomfortable situation for a therapist, but also demonstrates **motivation for change**, which is an important therapeutic condition. This is a far cry from Charles, who is doing all he can to protect his life from change and avoid therapy. Kristin's therapist can give immediate

attention to her desire for more in order to enhance the environment, while Charles' therapist will have to create a recognition of need before there is sufficient motivation for therapy.

Getting Charles motivated for change and therapy will probably include finding ways to cognitively challenge how well his choices get him what he wants. Discussions of how much he enjoys life and how real his anxieties are in relation to actual experiences are examples of conversations the therapist or daughter might encourage. Behavioural methods might include having his daughter stop bringing things to the house for him, thereby forcing him to deal with a need to move outside of his self-created cocoon. In this case, these techniques are designed to improve the facilitative environment by improving Charles' motivation to become actively involved in the therapeutic process.

The cognitive-behavioural approach to utilizing Kristin's obvious motivation would be to move quickly to identify and build upon what she wants changed about her life and therapy. This would form the basis for setting necessary goals and designing later experiments. No matter how obnoxious Kristin might get, she has offered the motivation for change and therapy that is required. It should be supported and put to maximum use.

Highlighting goals
In cognitive-behavioural therapy, the motivation to change and the highlighting of specific goals are closely related. Once clients have the motivation to change and come to therapy, the task of the cognitive-behavioural therapist is to clarify the essence of that motivation and turn it into logical, behavioural goals that can be realistically sought. If motivation provides the impetus for change, goals provide a clarification of the direction and extent of change. The most facilitative therapeutic environment is one in which both the impetus for and the direction of change are continually in evidence, since these conditions help keep the therapeutic process and the people involved in it clearly focused.

Establishing, revising and re-establishing goals plays a large part in the maintenance of an environment that facilitates therapeutic change as information, motivation and other conditions change. Initial goals based on limited understanding on the parts of both client and therapist are the places to begin, but rarely the places to end. Like many clients, Kristin's goals will probably begin as broad, vague concepts: 'I want more out of life', or 'I want you to be better than my past therapists'. These are acceptable starting places, but if they remain this vague for long, they will not provide sufficient sense of direction to allow her to observe the progress necessary to maintain motivation. Her therapist will thus work to clarify these initial broad goals and develop more specific sub-goals that will give better direction and more opportunity to predict potential outcomes as well as the means to reach them.

Which specifics, then, does Kristin associate with a better life and which ones are tied to the aspects of her current life that are most counterproductive? How does she think of herself and how does she want to think differently? What does she want to do and what does she want to stop doing? Where does she need more control in her life and where might she be better off giving up attempts to control? The more these goals can be connected to specific thoughts and behaviours, the more conducive the therapeutic environment will be to the exploration of new thoughts and actions.

Establishing a hypothetical mindset

Keeping an open mind is an essential ingredient for a facilitative cognitive-behavioural environment. Allowing alternative ideas and their potential influence to be given consideration is essential for exploration of life's possibilities and the potentials of therapy. A closed mind, on the other hand, limits or eliminates the core cognitive-behavioural processes of learning, unlearning and relearning from the therapeutic endeavour. Cognitive-behavioural therapists attempt to imbed the **open-mindedness** of the hypothetical mindset into therapy sessions by continually devising and exploring possible scenarios for later testing.

Consider statements that might be made by Charles and Kristin's therapists to maintain a hypothetical mindset:

> You are sure it would be terrible to go out the door. Charles, what would happen if we walked outside of the house together?

> Kristin, how would it change things for you, if you turned your chair so that you faced me?

The use of this kind of statement is perhaps most recognizable as a cognitive technique for challenging client beliefs. However, it also serves the environmental function of helping the client remain open to new potentialities by creating hypotheses that can be tested in thought, conversation and reality.

Creating a climate where hypotheses are continually developed to estimate outcomes based on the potential accuracy of beliefs is an essential ingredient in cognitive-behavioural therapy. Nothing Kristin does is denounced as wrong or verified as correct. Instead, her actions are considered with regard to the potential outcomes they might produce. Similarly, telling Charles what would or would not happen when he left the house would simply promote a closed-minded, 'facts-are-facts' approach to therapy. Either the therapist or the client would be seen as having the right answer and the only task would be for one side to accept the other without question. In contrast, creating an environment where continual questioning of all thoughts and actions as to their potential outcomes is the norm–promotes the essential hypothetical mindset necessary for exploration and experimentation.

Continuing experimentation
Cognitive-behaviour therapy demands an environment where hypothesized outcomes of thoughts and actions can be tested regularly. Without such an environment and without such testing, there would be no way for Charles or Kristin to know whether their old thoughts and behaviours were valid or whether new ones might work better. They must be willing to test old and new to judge the accuracy of the hypotheses they create from beliefs and observations.

Experiments can be cognitive or behavioural and they are used both inside and outside of therapy sessions, although most cognitive-behavioural experiments are cognitive in nature. For example, Charles might develop a hypothesis like the following:

Going outside even with you would be a disaster. The air is bad, cars wreck, and people are killed everywhere, all the time. Even if I wasn't killed it would be so horrible I would die.

The therapist, recognizing these concerns as illogical and exaggerated, could then provide a cognitive test of Charles' hypothesis along the lines of, 'Your daughter, myself and others won't die as soon as we leave your home, or will we? Will I die or will it just be you? Will you really *die*?'

Regardless of Charles' analysis of the outcome of this specific mental experiment, a facilitative stage will be set for others. Therapist and client can now move through a set of experiments where each one changes the hypothesis to some extent and alters the next experiment. Eventually these cognitive experiments logically progress into an obvious behavioural one, walking outside together.

Once Charles and the therapist, having gone outside, find that they both survive, a greatly altered hypothesis will have to be developed.

It will surely still be influenced by fear, anxiety and other potential disasters that Charles' mind can create so that not all his old reactions will disappear. Nevertheless, he will perceive things differently and the difference, although small, can be vital. Indeed, a number of small differences achieved through a series of experiments, each focused on testing a single hypothesis, have a cumulative effect that can far exceed any attempt to answer every possible form of a hypothesis once and for all with a single magnificent experiment.

Necessary experiments conducted within therapy sessions are not the end of therapy. Conditions must also be right for experiments to be carried out in the everyday world outside. 'Homework' is the term commonly associated with experiments held outside therapy. If Charles learns to leave the house with the therapist, he will have only gained in the context of therapy. Homework experiments must be designed for Charles to test his progress on his own and under circumstances more similar to those he experiences in everyday life.

Therapists have less control of conditions in the external environment than in therapy sessions and must, therefore, be more careful when designing experiments. Asking Charles to walk two miles in a crowded city every day would allow too many variable conditions to realize a true assessment of a hypothesis. Stepping out of the door and retrieving the paper once a day for a week would be a more reasonable experiment with a less variable and more facilitative environment. As each experiment revises the hypotheses, environmental constraints can be relaxed, since fewer and fewer specific conditions will be necessary to maintain an environment that facilitates hypothesis-testing and experimentation.

Building a reinforcing environment
The process of developing hypotheses, experimenting with them and revising them based on results can give validity to ideas and actions, but not necessarily establish the value of the results. Clients who make experimental changes need to have conditions available to support those changes. Progress for Kristin or Charles, for example, will be short-lived without an environment that reinforces the changes they *do* manage to make.

Therapists often start **building a reinforcing environment** by taking on the role of reinforcing-agent in therapy. Physical and verbal attending behaviours will support Kristin's involvement and facilitate additional data collection from her. Communicating approval when Charles rejects a self-defeating thought and replaces it with a more productive one provides a building block in the development of his reinforcing conditions. Thus words of reinforcement might be offered, such as, 'Yes, you seem to now see the problems your thinking has caused and the benefits of your new set of thoughts. That is a major accomplishment in itself!' An accurate and enthusiastic statement in this vein strengthens discovery and increases the chances of future positive steps occurring. Indeed, once Charles and Kristin realize that such reinforcements are readily available for appropriate thoughts and/or behaviours in therapy, the directed reinforcing condition will become a supportive portion of each session, even when no particular reinforcement is being provided to each and every action.

Other ways therapists attempt to build a directed reinforcing environment are by altering clients' internal cognitive patterns or external behavioural situation. Helping clients replace inaccurate and self-defeating thoughts with more appropriate and productive ones is an attempt to create a cognitive environment that facilitates directed reinforcement of productive thoughts rather than non-productive ones. Changing child discipline procedures, involving the wife of an alcoholic in his treatment, or scheduling daily relaxation time for the busy executive, all are behavioural attempts to produce a reinforcing environment more directly and consistently supportive of desired goals.

When Kristin eventually turns to face the therapist or Charles sits in front of the therapist, a directed reinforcing environment will be one where the look and words of the therapist will clearly support those actions. As a client's productive words and actions are reinforced in realistic and agreeable ways by the therapist, the client and others, the environment becomes more reinforcing and the need for each individual response to be behaviourally reinforced is reduced.

Instituting collaboration
Therapists know most about therapy and therefore have the greater responsibility for directing it. Clients know most about themselves and so have the greater responsibility for directing their lives. The result of these dynamics is that a facilitative environment must be consistent enough to promote the planned efforts of cognitive-behavioural therapists, yet flexible enough to incorporate client and therapist differences in knowledge and responsibility. The collaborative model of cognitive-behavioural therapists attempts to meet the need for consistency and flexibility by accounting for changes in the relationship over time.

The initial environmental need for Kristin and Charles, as seen by cognitive-behaviourists, is to learn about the process and accept it as one that can work for them. This confers key relational responsibilities of **teaching and persuasion** upon the therapist. In these early stages, the environment characterized by this kind of working relationship can be seen in the types of actions therapists employ:

- explaining the process clearly and in a language and a cultural context the client can understand;
- listening to the client to match information to be taught with the client's specific situation;
- assessing client abilities to learn so that teaching amounts and speed do not exceed abilities;
- offering examples of how the process has worked for others in similar circumstances;
- providing logical and printed evidence, and
- focusing the client on establishing goals and hypotheses and experimenting with them from the beginning of the process.

This early, directive, teaching environment changes over time as clients learn the process and accept responsibility for implementing it inside and outside of therapy sessions. It is expected that, as Kristin and Charles begin implementing the process for themselves, they will become even more convinced that it is working in their favour to create positive changes. Their therapists will reduce the directive-teacherly emphasis and take on more consultative functions in proportion to Kristin's and Charles' changes. This will create a more equal footing in an environment where Kristin and Charles develop their own goals, hypotheses, experiments and reinforcements, while the therapist becomes the consultant to them.

The progressive change in environment continues until such time as the consultant seems not to be needed sufficiently to warrant continuing contact. This time marks the appropriate end of therapy sessions for the present. There may well be an expectation, however, that additional teaching or consultation could be required in the future and that, if or when it is, there may be a need to return to therapy.

Enhancing relationships
The core conditions of a cognitive-behavioural facilitative environment emphasize logic, organization, planning, process and action. These technical factors receive much more emphasis in print than the personal and emotional aspects of the environment. Since the technical aspects are the ones that make cognitive-behavioural

therapy unique from other therapies, this emphasis in print should not be surprising. Research also tells us, however, that an environment where relationships are enhanced does make a difference in the effectiveness of the technical aspects (Burns and Auerbach 1996).

There are clear and reasonable connections between the technical and relational sides of cognitive-behavioural therapy. For example, therapist listening and observing can be considered technical actions designed to collect cognitive, environmental and emotional client-data. Therapist-responding logically follows listening to clarify accuracy of understanding and put the therapist in a more rational position to help develop appropriate goals, hypotheses, experiments and reinforcements. These listening, observing and responding actions, which promote the enhanced relationship condition, are the same ingredients that go into acquiring and demonstrating empathy in clients.

Professional ethics dictate that therapists should not lie and deceive clients and that they should be honest about the relationship. Yet the reasons for being honest are therapeutic as well as ethical. Creating a reinforcing environment, a part of which employs therapists themselves as personal reinforcers, means that therapist warmth and caring are important. Together with empathy, these relational conditions have been found to be valuable aspects of the therapeutic environment (Beck *et al.* 1993). Thus both Kristin and Charles will, to some extent, have their doubts about therapy reduced if they have a sense of being understood and cared about by their therapist. Believing that the therapist is 'in their corner' – understanding them, feeling for them and fighting *with* them – strengthens motivation to continue and confidence that they are not alone.

Therapists who appear to be 'real people' – that is, are genuine – rather than simply playing a role, also improve client confidence and motivation to continue working. Therapy is, in part, the putting aside of real day-to-day environments and relationships to work on issues from a different angle. This valuable aspect of therapy can also have its downside by producing an unrealistic environment where the connection to the real world may be questionable. **Therapist genuineness**, in addition to technical ability, empathy and warmth, can help guard against the potential unreality of the therapeutic environment by grounding it in a sound and realistic way of relating.

The relationship variable in cognitive-behavioural therapy is not the environmental variable that is thought to provide therapeutic change. It is, however, a variable that adds balance to the environment in ways that allow other techniques to have maximum effect.

Conclusion

The twentieth century has seen the blending of cognitive, behavioural and social learning techniques into what is most commonly referred to now as cognitive-behavioural therapy. Each orientation contributes to an overall approach that maintains a focus on unlearning and relearning through hypotheses generation, experimentation, data-results analysis and redesign of new hypotheses. The related therapeutic techniques clearly combine thinking and behaving in experimentally controlled ways to seek quantifiable outcomes. The therapeutic environment required to implement cognitive-behavioural therapies must, therefore, be one that provides the order, planning and relationships necessary to foster these semi-controlled scientific activities.

Although all cognitive-behavioural therapies have a consistent general focus on unlearning, relearning and scientific experimentation, variations between the therapies are as great as they are between those belonging to any other broad theoretical field. These variations manifest themselves most clearly in the ways in which therapists choose and implement therapeutic techniques. In contrast, commonalty can be seen most clearly in those conditions that constitute the facilitative environment and which are considered necessary for successful implementation of the various techniques. This chapter has focused upon those general facilitative environmental conditions that emerge regardless of the specific cognitive-behavioural therapy and its associated techniques.

A summary of the necessary ingredients for the facilitative cognitive-behavioural environment presented in this chapter pays close attention to several key interconnected components. The controlled, experimental nature of cognitive-behavioural therapies requires the environmental condition of 'order', the availability of client 'goals' sought, and the 'motivation' to accept that order and pursue those goals. These conditions allow for the logical collection, processing and analysis of the 'data' that is essential to the therapeutic process. Analysed data that reflect client ideas and behaviours need to be used in combination with additional environmental ingredients, including a 'hypothetical mindset'. This condition of mind encourages the testing of beliefs and behaviours through 'experimentation'. The most positive results of these experiments call for 'environmental reinforcement' for consistency to develop in the unlearning of less helpful cognitions and actions, and the learning or relearning of more helpful ones. The combination of these conditions and the techniques that utilize them also call for an environment of 'collaboration' between counsellor and client, which, in turn, demands attention to building a therapeutically 'enhanced relationship'.

The need for these key conditions that constitute a facilitative cognitive-behavioural environment remain generally constant whatever the therapeutic context. The specific nature and intensity of their presence, however, tends to change and evolve. For example, how much and what type of client motivation is essential will differ according to therapist, client, goals and situation, but the need for appropriate motivation to press forward with a therapist in an agreed-upon manner will not. Similar variations exist within the other facilitative environmental conditions and new variations will emerge as we continue to learn more about people and therapy. While changes like these are virtually a given, the present evolution of cognitive-behavioural therapy seems to confirm the general essential status of these basic facilitative conditions.

RESPONSE AND REFLECTION

NICK BARWICK

R.H. provides a broad perspective on the conditions which characterize the cognitive-behavioural environment. Some of these conditions, however, I see more as activities. My focus of interest is on what environmental conditions allow such fundamental activities to be undertaken effectively and used to therapeutic effect.

Increasingly, I believe, cognitive-behavioural therapists view the therapeutic *relationship* as providing the 'necessary' conditions (see, for example, Morris and Magrath 1983; Meichenbaum 1985; Beck *et al.* 1990; Ellis 1995; Lazarus 1995)[1] and it is upon the therapeutic *relationship*, therefore, that I should like to reflect. Specifically, I should like to make two brief excursions, focusing first on the influence of social psychology and second on the influence of post-rational, constructivist psychology on the attitude to and use of relational conditions in behavioural and cognitive-behavioural therapies. The former R.H. touches upon; the second, I think, he alludes to but does not elaborate.

The influence of social psychology
As R.H. suggests, first-generation behavioural therapists determinedly play down the significance of 'interpersonal interaction variables'

(the therapist–patient relationship) in the therapeutic venture (Eysenck 1960; Mowrer, 1964). Descriptions of therapist as 'behavioural engineer' (Allyon and Michael 1959) and patient as 'biological unit' (Wolpe 1958) intentionally strip the therapeutic encounter of human characteristics, leaving 'super psychotechnologists' (Meyer and Bartlett 1976) to implement programmes that appear to gain little from therapist–patient contact (see, for example, Glasgow *et al.* 1981). Yet, even from the outset, although clearly identifying technique as the means of effecting change, some behavioural pioneers explicitly recognize the importance of 'good rapport' (Wolpe 1954; Lazarus 1963) and of establishing a 'positive relationship' before technical intervention (Wolpe 1958).

Why, then, the difference? Why demote the import of relationship conditions in theory while attending to them in practice? Commentators suggest that it is because of the nature of the relationship. Being the outcome not only of observable behaviours but also of unobservable thoughts and feelings, it does not fit well with behavioural therapy's scientific methodology (Wilson and Evans 1977). Thus, although its therapeutic efficacy has been repeatedly demonstrated – useful at least for keeping patients in therapy and on-task (Alexander *et al.* 1976; Rabavilas *et al.* 1979; Persons and Burns 1985) – lacking an acceptable way of defining, measuring or operating it, it has, as a concept, been confined to the behavioural backwaters of theoretical neglect – that is, until social psychology provided just such a frame for thinking about it.

Social psychology makes available to behavioural therapists the language of social influence – a way of describing the 'interpersonal context' or conditions in which technique is practised and by means of which learning processes may be initiated and fulfilled. After all, why do some patients make use of techniques while others do not? Why, if patients already recognize the need to change, do they make changes *in* therapy and not *before* it? Questions such as these have led some therapists to surmise that what brings about change is not simply the application of technique, but its application in the right environmental conditions: social conditions that influence behaviour and which some patients, by themselves, seem incapable of producing. Therapy thus becomes 'a goal-directed use of social influence as a condition for the individual process of learning' (Schaap *et al.* 1993: 23); in short, a persuasive endeavour in which therapist is cast as 'persuader' and patient as he or she in need of 'persuasion' (Gelso and Carter 1985). Initially, this led to focusing on the enhancement of certain qualities of the persuader as a way of providing conditions necessary to promote learning. However, the activity of persuasion has come to be seen as less static and more as the product of dynamic processes of social interaction.

One model of social interaction behavioural therapists draw upon is derived from exchange theory (Thibaut and Kelley 1959; Homans [1961] 1974). This describes individuals as possessing 'resources' of varying perceived value (Foa and Foa 1980) and describes relationships between individuals as working according to economic rules of exchange and barter. It is an interpersonal interaction model that provides therapists with a complex understanding of how to establish, maintain and monitor relationship conditions by means of matching certain kinds of patient need to certain kinds of therapist social power (see Janis 1982; Strong and Claiborn 1982; Dorn 1986; Maddux *et al.* 1987, Heppner and Claiborn 1989).[2] Apt matching enables therapists to maintain patient motivation and momentum, circumvent patient resistance/reactance and act, at times, as a sophisticated type of 'social reinforcement machine' (Krasner 1962).

The influence of post-rational constructivist psychology

As R.H. points out, one outcome of the 'cognitive revolution' has been the new relational condition of parity enshrined in cognitive therapy's notion of 'collaboration'. In effect, the patient is warmly coaxed to play 'co-investigator' in joint experiments with the therapist (Beck and Weishaar 1995). R.H. also alludes to the fact that not all mainstream cognitive-behavioural approaches are quite so warm or egalitarian. Rational emotive (behavioural) therapy is, for example, more didactic, directive and confrontational. Indeed, aiming to 'attack' and 'demolish' patients' irrational thinking, Ellis (1995) warns against overt therapist warmth, suggesting it can reinforce problematic beliefs about the need to be loved by everyone (Ellis and Dryden 1997). However, whether relational conditions are collaborative or confrontational, these cognitive-behavioural therapies can both be seen as adopting strategies of persuasion (Guidano 1991) in an attempt to educate the patient about reality. This highlights the philosophical assumptions of realism and rationalism that underpin traditional cognitive-behavioural therapy.

Realism assumes the existence of a stable, external reality which is available to our senses[3] and which can be objectively verified. It is the job of the brain to process and store accurate representations of this reality. Rationalism echoes these assumptions, asserting that the superior method of dealing with and processing information about reality is by means of rational cognition. Consequently, the relational conditions sought are those deemed best suited to educating patients about this way of seeing and of processing what is seen.

Post-rational therapies (e.g. personal construct therapy, constructivist cognitive therapy, cognitive developmental therapy), however, question the assumptions of realism and rationalism and propose instead a 'relativistic' view. This view states that reality is neither stable nor objectively verifiable and that individuals construct reality as they construct themselves. In therapy, what needs to be assessed is not the validity of these constructs (logically tested against a given truth) but their viability. Furthermore, post-rational therapists question the unassailable primacy of cognition in processing experience and assessing what constructs arising from such processing are viable. Foregrounding other 'tacit' ways of knowing, both affective and unconscious processes are given equal status to cognition and seen as integral to our ways of 'construing'. Indeed, it is the capacity to 'process' creatively – to make new constructs, new meaning out of new experiences – which constructivists see as therapy's task to promote.

To promote a greater capacity to process creatively requires the patient's willingness to dismantle and reformulate those systems of meaning that have become petrified and impermeable to the influence of new experience (Kelly 1955). These systems are often 'core schemata': meaning-making systems that sustain identity and relatedness. Any change in them is of a 'second-order' nature (Lyddon 1990), requiring deep levels of intervention. Such interventions will inevitably meet resistance. This resistance is unlikely to be the result of patient–technique mismatch or lack of clear goals. Aptly dubbed 'security operations' (Safran and Segal 1990), it is seen by constructivists as the product of legitimate attempts to protect those core-ordering processes that are felt to be under threat (Neimeyer 1995b). Consequently, resistance is treated with respect, even reverence (see Leitner 1995).

This radical shift in understanding of the therapeutic task, of the processes that need to be vitalized to achieve it and of patient responses that might be expected to arise as a result of its pursuit, call for an equally radical shift in the relational conditions that allow such therapy to happen. First and foremost is the new weight given to conditions of safety and security. Indeed, some cognitive-behavioural therapists have drawn on attachment theory, normally associated with psychodynamic therapy (see Chapter 2), to explain the significance of offering patients a 'secure base' from which to explore painful aspects of identity (Guidano and Liotti 1985;

Mahoney 1991). Linked with this is the need for a delicate attunement to affect-laden events in the therapy, as these may provide evidence of core interpersonal schemata under threat. In short, although therapists must remain 'separate' from their patients and retain an observational, scientific stance, they must also cultivate and communicate an empathic 'connectedness'. This has been described as 'optimal therapeutic distance' (Leitner 1995). The dual nature of this stance allows therapists to recognize the 'pull' of the patient – feelings and 'action-tendencies' stirred up in the therapist by the patient through their behaviours – and yet 'unhook' from them so as not to be drawn into reinforcing the patient's 'interpersonal cycle' – their usual way of relating. Instead, the therapist 'meta-communicates' about these in-session events and helps the patient reflect on their source in interpersonal schemata, schemata that may be causing problems outside the therapy room (Jacobson 1989; Safran and Segal 1990; Liotti 1991).

Negative 'pull' can lead to 'alliance ruptures'. These are temporary breakdowns in the 'working alliance', a term widely adopted by cognitive-behavioural therapists and generalized from psychodynamic theory (see Bordin 1979). Traditionally, cognitive-behavioural wisdom suggests such ruptures are to be avoided. Post-rational cognitive-behavioural therapists, however, tend to see them as opportunities not only to gather 'experimental evidence' of unhelpful negative interpersonal schemata (Beck *et al.* 1990), but also to 'disconfirm' these schemata by means of alliance rectification (Robins and Hayes 1993). In this way, therapists hope to negotiate with their clients a state of 'authentic relatedness'[4] (Safran 1998). To this extent, post-rational, constructivist cognitive-behavioural therapy may be seen as going beyond its therapeutic forebears, in that not only does it deem the therapeutic relationship as providing *necessary* conditions for therapeutic change but, in instances such as these, *sufficient* conditions as well.

CHAPTER 4

Core conditions of the existential-humanistic environment

RICHARD HAZLER

Introduction: worlds apart in the same place

John was a large black prisoner who kept very much to himself. His physique, scars and brooding look all gave the impression of someone from a very different world from my own, and the prospect of counselling him alone in a locked prison cell felt a particularly foreboding one. Yet, once in therapy, he shared a very quiet, peaceful and trusting side that did not match his looks at all. Which, then, was the real world – the real John?

John quickly made progress at opening up, trusting and looking for better ways to deal with his life. Encouraged by the progress, it was a shock when, after a particularly productive session, a guard who was normally friendly to me surprised me with his anger: 'Haz, you must be sick to try and help that bastard!' He turned quickly, emphasizing his disdain for me, and stomped away. What was going on here? A record-search showed that John was in prison for raping a 13-year-old and there were similar charges for other cases in several states. The guard's emotions now became more understandable, while my own became more confused. How could I have liked this person? How could I have enjoyed working with him? How could I have been so ready to believe in him?

In our next session, before I had even said a word, John recognized the confusion in me. 'You found out about my past huh? Well fuck you!' As he got up to call the guard and leave, I instinctively moved to stop him, although I did not know how I managed to do so or why. The words that came out were unplanned but honest.

Wait! . . . I'm having trouble figuring out my own feelings, that's true. Maybe I'm not doing too well right now, but we've worked well together and you've helped me understand before. You can do that again. But I need your help to know you better and to be of more help. Give me a shot?

John was used to people's reactions when they found out about his horrific acts. The disdain in their faces, words and actions were too much for him to take, so he hid from people, both physically and psychologically. He despised himself for what he did when, periodically, he went out of control. But where could he turn for help? His actions were too despicable for people to show caring for him, or even for John to care about himself.

We discussed my reactions and John's own feelings about his behaviours, feelings that were many times more painful to explore than topics like how others felt about and treated him. These discussions helped to develop between us a positive therapeutic relationship that may not have made John into a model citizen, but did give him hope, new ways of looking at life, and more productive ways of interacting with others.

We were so very different: black man/white man, poor/middle class, condemned/trusted, imprisoned/free, friendless/loved. Even as we sat in the same cell, exploring issues and feelings together, we saw the world in such entirely different ways. Yet, somehow, we also came to recognize common feelings. This commonalty linked us, allowing me to see and to experience something of his unique way of looking at and being in the world. It is the therapist's willingness and capacity to experience the unique world-visions of another that makes it possible to create an environment designed to focus on the perceived world of the client, the phenomenological world. This chapter explores the kinds of conditions that constitute such an environment and considers the humanistic and existential rationale for their therapeutic efficacy.

Paradigms and perspectives

The records and reactions of therapists, guards, judges and witnesses drew an objective picture of John's interactions with the world. It is this observable picture that Aristotle, Galileo or Isaac Newton, with their scientific minds, would have confirmed as the 'real world'. In Western culture, it was only late in the nineteenth century that a new philosophical coalition began to form that would call this 'observable real world' concept into question and would begin creating, in its place, a more holistic picture of human beings.

In the early 1890s, theoreticians such as Christian von Ehrenfels (1859–1932), in his work with music, and Edmond Husserl (1859–1938), in his work with mathematics began to suggest connections between the observable and the unobservable. These two thinkers, each in their own way, theorized that there must be interconnected wholes (**gestalts**) more significant to understanding existence than any of the separate observable parts (Smith 1988). This 'gestalt' concept had an impact well beyond its field of origin, finding its way into publications on philosophy, science and psychology. Pressure was rising to look beyond the observable pieces of discrete information about a human being and to focus on exploring connections within the **interdependent whole** that formed the uniqueness of each individual.

Philosophers like Kierkegaard (1944) had already explored the concept of truth and fact from this more flexible perspective that varies with our human inconsistencies. Heidegger (1962) expressed how that exactness, suggested in a purely objective picture of a person, misses the realities, complexities and inevitable imperfections of existence. These and related existential ideas began to guide therapists away from the 'facts on file' towards the subjective qualities, sensations and perceptions of clients like John – their inner worlds – to get the most accurate picture of human existence.

There was now a direct challenge to the behavioural view – maintained by the medical and scientific professions – of people as objects to be understood, analysed and manipulated into changing (Bugental and Sterling 1995). A new model was forming in which the subjective reality of human confusion was acknowledged and validated and greater attention was given to factors that could not be seen or tested so directly. The acknowledged existence of the complex and confusing nature of human experience called for different therapeutic conditions, such as more patient involvement, more professional listening, increased conversation, longer therapy – both in terms of length of appointments and duration of treatment – and a search for new ways of exploring the individual inner worlds of patients.

In Europe, the main proponents of existentialism's contribution to therapeutic practice were analytic psychiatrists such as Ludwig Binswanger (1963), Medard Boss (1963), Paul Tournier (1957) and Victor Frankl (1963). The direction of their focus tended to emphasize theoretical conceptualizations of people, whereas in America much greater emphasis was given to experiential actions and the pragmatic day-to-day realities of life. These differences became even more marked under the influence of the philosophically related tradition of humanism. Carl Rogers (1942), James Bugental (1965), Eugene Gendlin (1962), Rollo May (1961), Abraham Maslow (1943) and Fritz Perls (1969) were among the American humanistic therapists proposing new applications of existential concepts, which were more action-oriented and less preoccupied with existential philosophy.

Victor Frankl made a major impact on both the European and American therapeutic world by making what is often considered the strongest and most personalized case for an existential view of the world in *Man's Search for Meaning* (Frankl 1963). The vivid pictures he drew of life and death in a Second World War concentration camp strongly argued that the **meaning of life** was not predetermined by past events or by others who might control some physical aspects of a person's current existence. People always have choices in how they perceive and live their lives, no matter how dire the circumstances. This concept of personal control brought an immediacy to the therapeutic environment where choices could be made 'now' (Frankl 1997). Clients, no longer seen to be irredeemably directed by the past or by others, did not need to wait passively for their future to arrive. Instead, they could take control of aspects of themselves by determining their own meanings of events and actions in their lives.

Eric Fromm (1941, 1947) and Carl Rogers (1951, 1961) were among American leaders who drew on existential philosophy to inform their humanistically oriented therapy. They viewed humans as having far greater potential than had previously been accepted, seeing them as stronger, more moral and with a greater capacity to take control of their lives. The path to understanding and making the best use of these qualities was seen as running through the subjective worlds of client and therapist. It was clients, not therapists, who possessed the true perceptions of their existence, and only through those perceptions could meaningful decisions be made and actions taken.

Existential-humanistic therapy has become a way of helping people deal with life's uncertainties and complexities. The environment needed to achieve this is one which is designed to facilitate the connection between observable/factual views of human environment and subjective human perceptions of their experiences. The conditions of this environment, promoting as they do access to individuals' current subjective experiences, continue to be given attention today by modern and post-modern theories, and have informed the work of therapists working in other therapeutic schools (Neimeyer and Mahoney 1995). It is this access to the unique and immediate subjective world of human beings, where change becomes possible because we know that what is done is done, but what is perceived of what is done can continue to change that is central to the existential-humanistic school of therapy.

Many therapists in the 1950s and particularly the 1960s moved away from the more formal therapeutic roles advocated by the psycho-analytic model towards roles more in keeping with the existential-humanistic approach, an approach in which goals, interactions and contracts were more flexible and jointly designed. This expanded sharing of responsibility and more relaxed roles led to greater variety and informality in the therapeutic environment. Therapist dress became more casual, seating less rigid, interactions more varied and outcomes more open-ended and less conforming to social norms.

Other evolving concepts further strengthened **democratization and freedom** within the therapeutic relationship. For example, Rogers promoted faith in a person's **self-healing potential**, moving therapists increasingly to listen, trust and share themselves with clients. Fritz Perls, working with his lesser known colleagues, Hefferline and Goodman (1951), emphasized an action-filled gestalt approach in which awareness of the current interpersonal environment between client and therapist became key to assimilating new information into personal perceptions and actions. Worries from the past and hopes for the future were regarded with disdain as they sought to deal with all aspects of the client-as-a-whole in the immediacy of a present in which the import of past and future could be minimized.

Rollo May's (1953, 1961) existential perspective injected the concepts of client ultimate responsibility, therapist presence with the client and confrontation into the mix of therapy. It was clients who they saw as the critical ingredient for success or failure and not the therapist alone. **Ultimate client responsibility for progress** also freed therapists to become more involved in the process as *people* and to do so in more creative ways. They now had a freedom for greater exploration of the relationship and the potential roles of the therapist in the relationship. This expansion of personal responsibility and investment on the part of both client and therapist became a key factor in the future development of the conditions needed for successful existential-humanistic therapy.

Greater opportunities to explore potential roles in the therapeutic environment also increased the importance of the person inside the therapist. Less constraints on therapist roles and greater importance given to human aspects of the relationship brought important pressures to bear on the therapist as a person (Bugental 1987). Providing the humanistic environment as described by the likes of Maslow (1968), Rogers (1961), Bugental (1978) and Yalom (1980) becomes, in many ways, more of a personal challenge than a professional one. The therapist who provides an environment where caring, compassion, authenticity, unconditional regard, respect and honesty are maintained, models a **personal humanism** rather than implements selected techniques (Kottler and Hazler 2001).

The evolution of existential-humanistic therapy has contributed a variety of concepts that are now seen to form the heart of the therapeutic relationship. Concepts such as 'empathy', 'trust', 'immediacy' and 'congruence' describe essential ingredients in that relationship – core conditions of the existential-humanistic environment. Acting in accord with these conditions creates meaningful psychological contact and it is this 'contact' that is *the* essential condition for therapeutic change. The formation of a therapeutic alliance incorporates all these environmental conditions and thus provides a platform for strategies that can help people find meaning in their lives and acquire the tools to explore that meaning in everyday life. It is a platform that requires the continual maintenance of its constituent core conditions to keep it stable.

Core conditions

What conditions might increase the chances of John growing in a direction where his best aspects mature and gain focus over the ones that cause him the most trouble? In the introductory chapter, Kristin took control of the therapeutic environment. Can Kristin's model work or must a different environment be created for her to explore her problems effectively? These are the questions that must be answered before help in overcoming life's hurdles can be provided. This section explores the answers to these questions by focusing on the 'core conditions' necessary for effective existential-humanistic therapy. These include trust, empathic understanding, personal encounter, immediacy, personal stories, patience, relationship commitment and the working alliance. Only when all these are in place can the wide variety of existential-humanistic techniques be employed to consistently help clients progress.

Trust
Existential-humanistic approaches place great confidence in the client's ability and motivation to make productive life-changing decisions

(Hazler 1999). This confidence is based on the construct that people are continually seeking growth and self-actualizing experiences in the world (Maslow 1954). It is a belief that gives each person credit – even a multiple rapist like John – for having the innate tendency to move towards actualization of personal potential in the most positive ways he or she can find. It is this **self-actualizing tendency** that the existential-humanistic practitioner seeks to support and free from the constraints placed on it by self and others.

Rogers (1977) has made the strongest case for the need to **trust in the human organism**. He views the evil apparent in humans as being essentially positive strivings distorted by the environment. It follows, he suggests, that given a sufficiently safe environment, a person's desire to move in positive directions will prevail. Rollo May (1969) reaches much the same practical conclusion, although he gets there by viewing the 'daimonic' forces in humans as being basically neutral. For him, negative forces only gain some control if they are not admitted into awareness. Common, then, to both Rogers and May is their trust in people's natural tendency to seek positive ends, and it is this trust that is a key condition for therapy.

Clients like Kristin and John are certainly difficult, but their therapists must have faith in them as human beings who are seeking and able to find a successful existence regardless of the nature of their current or past difficulties. This contrasts with other views of human nature that question whether people have the inherent will or ability to change in positive ways. The environment established by the existential-humanistic therapist is one that continuously demonstrates faith in the ability of the client to make good choices for themselves and for others.

Empathic understanding
Empathic understanding is a cornerstone of the existential-humanistic approach in that it makes concrete the therapist's faith in clients by seeking to understand the personal experience of their worlds (Rogers 1957). It reflects the belief that individuals respond to the world around them as they uniquely experience it, and not as others see it. This phenomenological perspective recognizes that events experienced by any two people are bound to be perceived differently (Rogers 1961). Two armies fight, two adults argue and relationships often break down because each side perceives what is 'right', although what is 'right' is different for each side. The subjective/ phenomenological conclusion deduced from these examples is that, although there may be a 'socially approved right' or an 'objective

right', each of these groups and individuals sees the world through a different lens. It is on the basis of what is seen through this lens that their words, behaviours, feelings and beliefs evolve.

The **phenomenological view** that each client possesses a different and unique perception of the world requires therapists to gain a personalized understanding of that world in order to provide effective therapy. Empathic understanding is a way of gaining such an intimate perspective. It is an experiential state through which 'therapists steep themselves in the world of the other attempting to understand how others see and experience themselves and their worlds' (Bohart and Greenberg 1997: 5–6). In short, it is a core condition for therapy, since it enables therapists to give direct attention to each client's uniquely perceived experiences.

The idea that no two people perceive the world in exactly the same way explains much of the variation we see in our two client examples. John views the world as threatening to the positive perceptions of himself. People's reactions to him and his own distaste for the worst of his actions focus attention on the negatives and totally miss the positives. In other words, the healthy part of John's perceived world is only available within him and not commonly available to others. To use that healthy part for positive motivation requires the therapist to enter John's phenomenological world.

Kristin perceives threat in the environment that her therapist has provided. To protect herself, she acts in ways that might logically, according to her own subjective view of things, defend her from some of that threat. An existential-humanistic therapist would attend to Kristin's and to each client's uniquely perceived world and, working hard to understand that world, seek to help clients grow through their unique perspective, rather than only through the world perceived by therapists or others.

Entering the client's world from their perspective is no easy task, as we saw in the example from John's sessions. Had I known of John's background before working with him, could I have put aside my socially approved biases about this man's behaviours? It is hard to set aside our biased views in an attempt to see things through the client's eyes, but without doing so we treat clients from our own perspective and not from the perspective of the psychological world they inhabit. Continual acting on inaccurate perceptions of the client's world creates a situation where client and therapist go in different directions. Empathic understanding allows practitioners to select directions and techniques that give maximum attention to the world as the client experiences it.

Personal encounter

During its development, existential philosophy may have, at times, discounted the critical quality of **meaningful encounters** with others (Tageson 1982), but the humanistic movement has made this factor a core condition for the modern practice of existential-humanistic therapy. Martin Buber ([1958] 1970) suggests this **I–Thou relationship** is critically different from the **I–It relationship**, only the former providing the necessary conditions for growth to be achieved. It therefore becomes essential that client and counsellor have their phenomenological worlds connect directly (I–Thou), rather than only having the client's existence examined while ignoring the therapist's as though he or she were more a therapist than a person (I–It).

Perls *et al.* (1951: 230) pushed the I–Thou concept further by convincing many of his core beliefs that, 'All contact is creative adjustment of the organism and environment'. He proposed that all the factors interacting in one's immediate environment are critical for growth and that they can be accessed most directly and effectively only in highly **personal contacts** with others. The best connection was therefore one that was fully immediate and involved all thoughts, feelings and actions of both client and counsellor.

One could see these highly personal encounters simply in terms of two people being in physical proximity. This is an external view. Existential-humanistic therapists, however, view such an encounter as far more complex than this and seek to utilize its complexity accordingly. Perls (1976), for example, describes this interpersonal dimension in terms of **boundaries** located where the internal workings of the individual come into contact with the external environment. Effective therapy accesses those boundaries where psychological events occur between two or more people in the form of an observable combination of emotions, thoughts and actions. These boundaries cannot be found alone, but require two or more people to create the potential for a positive chain of psychological events that builds awareness and allows for positive change.

Therapeutic psychological contact is promoted most directly by the therapist's ability to reflect the client's thoughts, feelings, words and overall experiences. Many early humanistic therapists misinterpreted Rogers' concept of verbal **therapeutic reflection** as a directive to leave the 'person' of the therapist out of the contact. Yet Rogers saw reflection not as a set of verbal responses, but as a holistic way of testing understandings with the client.

I am not trying to 'reflect feelings'. I am trying to determine whether my understanding of the client's inner world is correct – whether I am seeing it as he or she is experiencing it at this moment. Each response of mine contains the unspoken question, 'Is this the way it is in you? Am I catching just the color and texture and flavor of the personal meaning you are experiencing right now? If not, I wish to bring my perception in line with yours.'

(Rogers 1986a: 376)

Reflection in action is demonstrated by therapists being **authentic** and by their recognizing and acting upon internal reactions during therapy in response both to observations and to the client's phenomenological perspective (Rogers 1961). It is this reflective aspect of human contact that shows both understanding of the client and also adds original or newly understood interpersonal information to the relationship through the presence of the therapist.

Encounter rarely appears in a simple one-sided format. Kristin took some control of the relationship between herself and the therapist by limiting their physical and psychological contact. On the other hand, she also came to the therapist's office and engaged in some talking, which also allowed a significant amount of contact. The question from the existential-humanistic perspective is not whether there *is* contact, but will there be *enough* to allow troublesome therapeutic boundaries to be approached successfully?

Immediacy
Maintaining positive contact requires that both client and therapist give attention to their immediate interactions with each other. Just as John was ready to leave the therapy session when he perceived a change in the therapeutic relationship, so did Kristin's actions and words express clear doubts about the future of her relationship with the therapist. For these relationships to have a chance to progress, close attention must be given to their moment-to-moment state. This kind of attention gives rise to the condition of **immediacy**: a relational condition, the quality of which can be assessed by considering how directly client and therapist deal with each other in the **here-and-now** (Prouty 1994).

Sharing thoughts and feelings about problems, issues and each other as they occur are the basic mechanics of immediacy. These timely actions let client and therapist know what is currently happening, so that a full awareness of information and process can be maintained.

Attention to the 'Here-and-Now' (Yontef and Simkin 1989) and to
focusing on bodily reactions rather than words (Gendlin 1996) are
two of the many existential-humanistic concepts which give primary
attention to the immediate holistic environment. Without this continuing currency of understanding, implicit, but not directly stated,
thoughts can be missed and covert ideas and actions can take control.
Indeed, a lack of immediacy can cause therapist and client to begin
working at cross-purposes. As a result, distancing occurs and the
quality of the relationship is diminished (Cormier and Cormier 1991).

Immediacy thus keeps the changing nature of the client–therapist
relationship in focus. It allows clients and therapists to judge their
actions from minute to minute, thereby having the greatest chance
of changing the relationship for the better. It also gives permission
and even encouragement for expression of the client's emotions
related to their experience, since it allows to show, in the present,
what direct personal impact the experiences of both past and present
have. In this way, the changing nature of these experiences becomes
immediately available in the counselling environment where it can
be given direct attention.

John and Kristin both gave clear signals that they would cease
therapy quickly unless something specific happened. They had immediate concerns about counselling and therapists, as well as their
own safety, and were poised to end the relationship. The existential-
humanist's direct attention to the immediacy of these situations
strengthens the involvement of clients in the continuing evolution
of the narratives which constitute their personal life stories.

Personal stories
Empathic understanding, psychological contact and immediacy each
require that attention be given to the **personal stories** of clients.
Who individuals were, who they are, who they want to be and who
they can be requires the telling, reflecting, constructing and joint
understanding of their perceived experiences. Within these stories
lie the **essential patterns of thoughts, feelings and actions** that
describe who the psychological person is, how they became that
way and what guides their choices (Neimeyer 1995a).

The telling of individual stories often makes the difference between
whether logic prevails in determining a person's choices or whether
missing story pieces are left to control decision-making and actions.
A common, everyday example of this is evident in the difficulty
people have with weight loss. Among people who have ample access
to a wide variety of foods, weight problems are common. For nearly

all of those who are overweight, the logical solution is simple: eat less and exercise more. As straightforward as this solution is, most people who try to lose weight either fail or lose the weight and then gain it back. What stops them, then, from following such a simple and logical solution? Why does therapy for this problem have such limited success for some and fail for so many? The answers can be found in clients' personal stories: stories that direct their actions more profoundly than simple logic; stories that make each person's understanding of life different and that create change as life-long story-lines are revised.

Post-modern thought has developed this often unnamed, but always used, core condition into a better defined model. Emerging under the title 'narrative therapy', it recognizes that immersion in people's life stories helps us recognize how a person can be blind to obvious alternative actions or views that others would identify immediately (Monk *et al.* 1997). Full recognition of those blind spots, no matter how obvious they might be to others, requires an environment emphasizing the seeking of stories before specific efforts can or should be made to change interpretation or actions.

Problematic human stories, by their very nature, have **imbedded contradictions** that can help identify where changes need to be made. John is both a rapist and a kindly person. Kristin takes control of therapy at the same time as she demands that the therapist take responsibility. These obvious contradictions identify themselves through specific points or patterns within client stories. Where did the contradictions arise? What keeps them intact? Why aren't they recognized and challenged more effectively? Existential-humanistic therapists, in various ways, bring attention to these contradictions by closely involving themselves in the continuing development of clients' stories. It is this process that allows clients and therapists to recognize when they are perceiving **discrepant perspectives** of the same stories (Angus and Rennie 1989).

Combining trust, empathic understanding, contact and immediacy is the way therapists become healthy participants in the evolution of client stories. Discrepant perceptions are identified and explored to seek as much joint understanding as possible. **Common perceptions** are confirmed as joint understandings that should strengthen the relationship and the ability to work towards changing discrepant perceptions. The stories are a core condition of therapy that allow for the accurate development of a **shared frame of reference**. This frame can be used to reconceptualize old stories and create new, more productive ones.

Patience
Client personal stories are like mysteries. They attract us with their intricacies and complexities, their twists and turns of plot. The best mystery stories force us to rethink and revise initial perceptions of what is happening and why as the story progresses. Obvious problems surface quickly, but we accept the idea that other problems will show themselves to be even more critical as the story unfolds. Following the story through to the end is the only way to put all the pieces together and that takes patience on the part of the reader or listener.

Time is needed to unravel the complexities in client stories, just as it takes time to follow the detail of the twists and turns in a mystery novel. The difference is that clients, unlike readers of a novel, do not have the acceptable novel ending worked out in advance. Following a client's story takes **patience** on the part of therapists (Monk *et al.* 1997), often to an extent we would not choose if we had the choice.

Limited funds, managed care and the desire for clients to find better lives tend to pressure both clients and therapists to move more quickly in therapy than is often either possible or advisable (Kottler and Hazler 1997). We may see things in clients from our personal contexts that make us want to tell them, 'just do it this way' or 'change that thinking'. Clients also often want immediate answers to problems without having to struggle through the whole story. Yet the complexity of human beings and the existential nature of existence simply do not allow for such quick and successful conclusions. Clients and therapists must patiently explore the full story as it emerges with its multitude of twists of plot, **unseen problems and hidden strengths**.

Existential-humanistic therapists try to move their clients' stories along quickly, but only as quickly as is appropriate. This means having the patience to recognize clients' need to pace themselves. Impatience in the therapeutic relationship reduces the necessary safety for both client and therapist (Watson and Greenberg 1994), resulting in less positive potential for therapeutic change. On the other hand, the ability to move at a **pace** complementary to that of the client creates an environment where more effective therapy can take place (Kottler 1991).

Clients have taken their whole lives to create personal ongoing stories, and these stories are unlikely to change as quickly as the objective observer might expect. Clients need time to tell them; time to recognize the contradictions; time to think through the implications; time to try out new thoughts and actions; and time to rework old, less productive narratives into new, more productive ones. It is a turbulent process in which every new piece of information changes the emerging story and suggests new perspectives that demand attention. Patience is required to accept a slower pace than might be desired. In effect, this means that both therapist and client must make a major commitment to the therapeutic relationship so that the necessary balance of pace and patience can be maintained.

Relationship commitment

The essential ingredients of an existential-humanistic therapeutic environment are centred around the development of a **therapeutic relationship**. Rogers and his followers suggest that 'the process of therapy is synonymous with the experiential relationship between client and therapist' (Rogers 1951: 172). On the whole, gestalt therapists have similar views about the relationship, seeing it as the source of healing (Hycner and Jacobs 1995). However, not all existential-humanistic therapists recognize this totality of importance. Greenberg (1983: 146), for example, speaks for many who feel that while the relationship is 'essential to therapy, a good relationship is not seen as sufficient for therapeutic change'.

Although existential-humanistic therapists express noticeably different views about the relative import of the relationship factor, these differences are overshadowed by the consistencies they attribute to the nature of the relationship (Frank 1999). For example, existential-humanistic therapists seek engagement in an **authentic relationship** between client and therapist, where trust and mutual understanding develop through the sharing of moment-to-moment experiences (Kottler *et al.* 1994). Clients and therapists must therefore clarify and affirm their **commitment** to this relationship for therapy to progress effectively.

One of a therapist's worries about Kristin might understandably be that she is ready to bolt from the relationship at any time. She has physically and verbally positioned herself to leave at a moment's notice if she does not believe the relationship is going the way she desires. The therapist is being asked to 'prove' his investment in the relationship before Kristin commits.

The development of client commitment is a part of the process that needs to take place in most therapy sessions, although that need is not always evident in such a dramatic way. Prouty (1994) describes this process as one of **personal role investment**, where client and therapist must work with the dynamics of engagement versus detachment and therapist credibility versus uncertainty to develop the appropriate **therapeutic bond**. The therapist's role is to create such an investment on the part of both participants as to make sufficient joint commitment possible.

Working alliance
A **working alliance** in existential-humanistic therapy can be defined as being the solidification of the core conditions described above into a productive relationship for therapy. This solidification leads to an agreement between therapist and client on the key roles and responsibilities needed to work for progress in a collaborative partnership that will facilitate therapy. Aspects of personal or business roles are put aside and other therapist- and client-related roles are agreed in order to promote client progress (Kottler *et al.* 1994).

Kristin was personally anxious about allowing her therapist to direct their relationship. Her therapist wanted to demonstrate faith in her, but was also fearful that he might lose her or be hurt by her if he did not get her to interact in new ways that were more productive for therapy. I, as John's therapist, felt personal revulsion at his actions and this threatened to interfere with the therapeutic interactions. As for John, personal experience taught him to keep his negative side out of relationships with others in case they turned on him. These examples show how both clients and therapists must mutually agree to play certain roles even when they have strong desires to the contrary (Clarkson 1995).

Applications

Using case studies to examine existential-humanistic theories raises several problems. The standard case study model suggests that a collection of historical factors should be used to describe and diagnose an illness. Existential-humanistic practitioners have two major disagreements with this. First, they disagree that there are such things as 'absolute facts' to be placed in mental, paper or computer files. Existential-humanistic practitioners choose to place their emphasis on individual clients' perceptions of and feelings about their world as opposed to the facts as observed by others. The second problem relates to how the use of diagnosis promotes a medical model of identifying illness and removing the pathogen, while existential-humanists prefer a more health- and growth-oriented model of assessment and treatment. These differences result in existential-humanistic therapists focusing on the client–therapist relationship as a critical factor contributing to therapeutic success rather than on the elaboration of a client's specific, historically based case-diagnosis. Existential-humanistic practitioners attend closely to their clients because they want to understand their perceived experiences as fully as possible and to communicate clearly that understanding back to their clients. They utilize the core facilitative conditions to create an environment where shared understanding of physical, visual, emotional and verbal messages can be recognized and used. This deep understanding then becomes critical in creating a therapeutic relationship that is unique to the particular phenomenological world shared by client and therapist.

Any practical application of the existential-humanistic approach to creating core conditions for facilitating therapy begins with the potential phenomenological aspects of the client's situation. As would be expected with clients entering therapy, Kristin and John each have phenomenological views of the world that are **incongruent** with other feelings, abilities and potentials available to them. The incongruencies have grown throughout their lives as a result of the influence of cultural, familial and personal relationships. These developments have diminished their faith that the feelings, thoughts and actions of themselves and others can be trusted to be productive. What is needed is the creation of an environment where an awareness of these incongruencies is freer to emerge and where potential solutions – more congruent ways of being and behaving – become both available and viable.

Creating trust
People find it easy to say 'trust me', but much harder to implement the conditions which facilitate the earning and giving of trust. There are no basic phrases to use or actions to take. A trusting atmosphere is created through consistently displaying faith in others and in oneself.

Kristin's threats and doubts about therapy must be accepted for what they are and not discounted by therapist words or actions. The existential-humanistic therapist must demonstrate a belief that she is doing what she needs to do and that she will continually seek better ways of being. By giving Kristin the freedom to act in her chosen ways, the therapist demonstrates faith in her and in the relationship.

The existential-humanistic therapist will allow Kristin to choose the physical position of her chair no matter how awkward it is for therapy. Her doubts about the therapist and therapy will be explored through her stories rather than explained away by the therapist. To build Kristin's initial level of trust, it is more important to actively show faith in her ability to point out what is significant in the relationship and follow her lead. The urge to create what the therapist feels is a better situation must be put on hold until the levels of trust are raised enough for the therapist to offer alternatives without Kristin feeling that her ideas will be rejected.

Creating trust does not end with showing confidence in the client. Kristin's therapist must also trust himself and the therapeutic process. This trust in oneself and the process requires time and experience for therapists to try out new ways of being and evaluate the results. Doubts will obviously be raised in the therapist about whether this process will work if he proceeds to use Kristin's choice of relationship model. The therapist must believe in their joint ability to find suitable ways of both accepting her needs and blending them with his own and the needs of therapy. He must trust that formal training and personal development will facilitate thoughts and actions that will be flexible and creative enough to find effective interactions.

Kristin and John must develop productive levels of trust in themselves, their therapists and the therapeutic relationship. Coming to the sessions is a first sign that some level of trust – enough to make a beginning – is available. Seeing and hearing that the therapist has a model for working and that such a model has worked with others should support and expand that trust.

For both therapist and client, trust grows to the extent that each perceives the truth in the other person's words and actions. Being consistent in doing what you say you will do is a key contribution to establishing trust, particularly the client's trust for the therapist. Doubt becomes stronger as inconsistency reduces the potential for the other person in the relationship to know what is coming next or what future actions to take. The more the therapist and client see that what they expect from the other actually comes to pass, the greater will be their **faith in the process**, their willingness to give their true selves to it and their belief that a full, personalized understanding will emerge.

Producing empathy
Empathic understanding has two dimensions essential to making it a useful construct: understanding and accurately conveying that understanding. The first step is to set aside personal beliefs and enter the other person's world for maximum understanding. To do this, therapists must be flexible enough to leave behind their well-developed opinions, value-judgements and prejudices.

Tīng
(Tīng is the Chinese symbol for Listen)

'Listening' is the common term used to describe the most obvious way of gaining empathic understanding, but it is a term that describes an activity that goes far beyond the hearing of sounds and the registering and remembering of words. The Chinese symbol for listening (**Tīng**) offers a better representation of the existential-humanist's perception of this complex activity than the English definition does. Separate parts of Tīng refer to the ears (耳), eyes (目), the heart (心) and emphasize undivided attention. The Chinese recognize that this kind of listening is much more than the simple 'hearing' definition so often attributed to it.

Words can communicate cognitive information well but they do not always express emotions as successfully as other modes of communication, be they vocal or physiological. Prosodic features such as speed of delivery, pitch, tone, intonation and volume may all communicate emotions in ways that could go unexpressed in the words themselves. Similarly, facial expressions, tears, laughter, body position and physical movements can also complete a verbal story and modify the impact it is having in the present moment.

Frequently, the most productive factor in gaining empathic understanding is the therapist's sensitive awareness and use of the **interplay between words, voice, face and physical movements**. For example, the most complicated or troubling aspects of client stories are often distorted or hidden by the words used rather than clearly communicated by them. The distortions this incongruent use of words induces are unlikely to be corroborated by all of the client's other communicational modes. In contrast, word usage that *is* congruent is more likely to be complemented by vocal, facial and other physical communications. Empathic understanding is gained by attending to all these communicational modes to create the most accurate picture of the client's world.

Reflective encounters
Just understanding a person's world is not sufficient for establishing a facilitative environment. A more active contact is required to

operationalize the understanding. People must receive sufficient active feedback if they are to be made aware that they are understood, if they are to be able to acknowledge what is understood about them, and if they are to be enabled to judge how accurate and extensive that understanding is. The most common term used for describing this process of showing understanding is **active reflection**.

Reflection, like listening, is seriously under-utilized when it gives attention to spoken content only. Karon and VandenBos (1981) identify separate types of 'contact reflections' for use with clients with schizophrenia. Situational reflections, word-for-word reflections, facial reflections and body reflections each provide different ways of making reflective contact with all clients. Each one directs the therapist to give attention and reactions to a different aspect of the client's experience and the understandings between client and therapist. Together they create a more comprehensive attention to all information the client and client/therapist together have available to them.

Situational reflections focus on the client's mode of interaction. At some point in a session with Kristin, for example, her therapist might find a need to say, 'It is hard to hear you when you speak away from me'. This reflection gives situational context to the interaction of the therapy session. Similar reflections can prove beneficial when discussing other issues or interactions within sessions or outside the therapy room. An example of a situational reflection which focuses on interactions outside the office might be, 'So you feel like you have almost no friends, yet you stay at home and avoid contact with people'. Here the therapist reflects a contradiction, presented by the client, between what appears to be an unsatisfying situation – a lack of friends – and actions that promote that situation – avoiding contact.

Word-for-word reflections can be used to confirm a client's statement or to gain assurance that the specific words did in fact convey the desired meaning. Select words, phrases or whole sentences can be used. For example, a client might say, 'It feels like the first time I have really accomplished something important!' The therapist's understanding of the key message communicated might be demonstrated by reflecting, 'really accomplished something! It is a good feeling, isn't it?'

Facial reflections provide important information about those emotions that may not show up in the words of a client's story. A therapist might say, 'You look scared', 'You appear happy' or 'You have a smile on your face'. When these facial reflections match the verbal story being told, they are confirming; when they do not match, they point up contradictions.

The therapist can also provide facial reflections without words. By matching the client's facial expression, therapists can reflect back what is being seen. One client recognizing the cheerfulness of her therapist's face said, 'Why are you looking so cheerful about my problem?' The therapist replied, 'You are smiling and speaking in a cheerful voice as though it is humorous'. Again, such a reflection, arising out of observing the client's face, serves to highlight an incongruity in the client.

Body reflections can serve much the same purpose as facial expressions. Matching the client's body posture or movement can confirm their views or cause them to question their messages. One common therapy experience is for clients to change body posture and lose eye contact during difficult periods in a session. Simple reflection of these physical changes can be much less threatening than suggesting some issue is being avoided. It can also provide a clear indication of direct personal connection between therapist and client.

Making contact through various forms of reflection allows therapists to show understanding of their clients in multiple ways. This strengthens their connections and models positive interpersonal communication strategies. The result is that reflective contact helps sort out pieces of past stories while bringing their information and effects to the present therapy interaction.

Maintaining immediacy

The existential-humanistic approach places great power in the hands of clients, trusting their capacity to choose their actions even though they cannot control all that will happen in life. This emphasis on trusting the client's capacity to choose and to take the necessary action for him or herself requires that most of the energy of the therapeutic endeavour is channelled into the present – the only time one can make choices and take actions. Past experiences have a place in discussions, as do thoughts of the future, but therapists must seek ways to bring information about past and future back to the here-and-now for it to affect the present.

The most important tool for existential-humanistic therapists in returning sessions to the here-and-now is the therapy relationship. As John began to consider and discuss his past episodes of rape, he explained that he did not want them to be known because, 'No-one will ever care about me after knowing that stuff. There is just no hope to try and make my life work.' I reacted to John's comments with an immediate example of our relationship, 'But I am still here. You know we talk. You know I like lots of things about you. You know we feel good about our time together and believe it is useful. This doesn't seem to match your idea that there is nothing good left in life for you.'

This interaction did not change John's world forever, but it did bring a horrific past that appeared headed towards a hopeless future into a more productive, positive and hopeful present. This was the here-and-now where we were able to look at what was good in our relationship. These positive aspects could then later be expanded and related to his experiences of other people and situations as John's personal life-story continued to evolve.

Finding threads and holes in personal stories
The most valuable parts of clients' personal stories are not the different parts of the content, but instead the **conceptual threads** that run throughout and the holes where the stories become confusing. It is the threads that define a person much more than any specific event, no matter how interesting or tragic that event might be.

Kristin has had traumatic experiences in her life, but her behaviours with the therapist did not come from any single event. Her interactions with previous therapists played one part in her reactions, while her patterns of thinking and picturing how to get along in the world started much earlier. Parents, relatives, acquaintances, society in general and her own choices moulded interaction patterns that she felt offered the best ways to think and act. Identifying and exploring these patterns as they appear in the present will be much more the work of the existential-humanistic therapist than the focus on any single event, action, thought or decision.

The holes in personal stories are those places where the picture of how one event or belief leads to another begins to break down. My initial work with John highlighted a gaping hole, where a friendly, quiet person with a loving family was somehow connected to a person who had become a major threat to society. Only as a more complete version of these two separate narratives emerged did they come closer together in ways that began to fill in the hole.

Learning of the rapes that brought John to prison filled in some holes and opened many others. The 'loving family' was not the whole story. Rejection and abuse mixed with over-attention and protection created story threads that could only surface because the holes were recognized and given attention. The story of every client who comes to therapy is, like John's, more complex than it originally appears. As such, the exploration of its holes and threads requires attention, time and patience.

Complementary patience
Existential-humanistic patience does not mean waiting forever for the client to move or to take major initiatives. It is true that trust and faith in the client are demonstrated by therapist patience. Client personal stories take time to evolve and then more time to change. The truth in these statements is obvious, but viewed alone they leave out an important complementary aspect of the therapeutic relationship, the therapist as a forward-moving factor in the client's personal story. The effective therapist is one who uses a complementary form of patience that attends both to the client and therapist in relationship as well as to the client alone.

Clients are either in a hurry to 'get fixed' or are hesitant and want to go agonizingly slowly. It is the therapist's role in the relationship to follow the client's lead in terms of pace while also injecting their own understanding of what may be needed. The task is continually to test the limits of how much progress can be made while respecting the boundaries set by clients. The process becomes complementary when clients can see that their pace is being accepted at the same time as the therapist's professionalism is helping them to use time and energy wisely.

Complementary patience presses clients to go as fast as they can while allowing change to take place at the speed they choose. It is also a process that lets clients know where less patience might be valuable. Clients get to make choices and therapists help them to evaluate outcomes and reassess the speed of change being implemented. It is a process that uses the relationship to provide information and help evaluate the outcomes of client choices.

Committing to relationship roles
Commitment to a therapeutic relationship begins with the initiation of contact and expands from there to **investment in the people and process** of therapy. Clients make active commitment to seek help when they ask for therapists' time and therapists confirm their own commitment to help by agreeing. Future meetings must expand these initial steps to defining what help will look like in the relationship. What will be the responsibilities and expectations of each individual?

Agreement on roles and structures in existential-humanistic therapy is rarely set down in writing or in any other formalized way. Common working commitments are arrived at both by direct and indirect communication about how therapy is working, what would make it better and what changes need to be made. The concepts of change, growth, autonomy and trust are so elemental to existential-humanistic therapy that no absolute structure of roles, time-frames or frequencies of therapy would fit the unlimited variations in people and their changing perceptions and needs. The result is that commitments evolve with the changing needs of client and therapist in a relationship.

Existential-humanistic therapists communicate basic necessary commitments immediately and introduce new ones as they become necessary. Kristin, for example, has come to therapy and is ready to talk, although only on her terms for now. The therapist is accepting of her initial commitment, but his anxiety is raised by the fact that she will have to commit in other ways as therapy continues. How long does he wait to explore additional commitments? How does he communicate the commitments needed? These are the questions that must be answered as the therapist attempts to balance the commitment Kristin is currently offering with how much will be needed later in the relationship. What she offers seems acceptable for now, so the therapist moves at a pace Kristin can accept, but with the recognition that they must also move towards expanded commitments in the future.

Therapists must also offer their own commitment to the relationship and the process. Existential-humanistic therapists continually display their belief in their clients and in themselves. They must know their own reactions and biases to judge when, where and how to insert them into the relationship mix. I recognized my revulsion at learning of John's inexcusable behaviours. I wanted desperately to keep them out of the relationship, although at the same time I knew they would have to be some part of the relationship. John recognized their effect on the relationship even before I was willing to admit it. Denial of them would have simply shown John that I would avoid the truth when convenient, at the same time as I was advocating trust and honesty from both of us.

I allowed John to know of my revulsion, but I also allowed him to know of my confusion about these two disparate pieces of him. This was not all there was in me, but it was enough to give us something to work with when the relationship was on shaky ground. We committed to continue working together, knowing that more of my feelings and concerns would come out later when they might better fit the situation and the strength of our overall alliance.

Alliance for progress
The working alliance in an existential-humanistic context is not a specific factor as much as it is an amalgamation of all the other

factors. This is the point where trust, contact, patience, personal stories, empathy, immediacy and commitment to the relationship come together in an alliance for progress. It is the therapeutic relationship that develops from mixing the right human ingredients in the best proportions within a pair of joined mixing bowls.

Client and therapist form an existential-humanistic relationship that touches many parts of each person and allows those parts to be shared within the encounter. A variety of techniques and models are then used to make use of this wide-ranging interpersonal encounter. No matter what techniques are used, however, it is the core relationship ingredients that provide the foundation that techniques require for effective implementation.

Conclusion: an environment of communion

The existential-humanistic therapeutic environment is one where a communion of words, feelings, ideas and perspectives becomes achievable. Client and therapist bring their separate lives, bodies, minds and experiences together in ways that allow them to share their uniquely perceived worlds and learn from the communion between them. No attempt is made to blend the two worlds into one or to change one into the other. Instead, a meeting place is arranged where people with separate world perspectives can examine each other for better understanding of themselves and also themselves in relation to others. It is an environment that communicates much respect for differences, belief in commonalties and a commitment to learning and growing through the communal experience of therapy.

Existential-humanistic therapists bring all their training and professionalism to the encounter with clients, but it is their 'personhood' and the human relationship they can offer that provides the most unique aspects of this therapeutic environment. Therapy is an interaction between two people struggling to find more clarity and then taking actions to better deal with the meaning of their existence. The therapist is the person with more training in how to advance the struggle in positive ways, while the client is seeking help to implement the process. Client and therapist will each struggle to understand the other and themselves and it is within this struggle that growth emerges.

There is *no one world* in existential-humanistic philosophy and so there will likewise be *no one absolute therapeutic environment*, although there are clearly common elements. Two people will come into contact to work on finding the right mix of personal ingredients for successful therapy. The environment must include the give-and-take of empathic understanding to benefit from the contact between two worlds. The immediacy of contact and interaction provides the active environment needed to make decisions and take actions. There must be opportunity, willingness and patience to hear, explore and expand on the personal stories of those involved. These stories have not developed in days, will not be understood within minutes and must be given time to unravel.

It takes great commitment to the personal nature of the existential-humanistic therapeutic relationship for a productive environment to be created. It is a commitment that demands more than the therapist's proffering of information and skills. It demands, from both client and therapist, the commitment of the 'person' within. Only when client and therapist can make that commitment – a commitment to form a professional and personal working alliance over time – will an environment be created that maximizes those opportunities for the struggle and growth that are necessary for existential-humanistic therapy to succeed.

RESPONSE AND REFLECTION

NICK BARWICK

No other therapeutic orientation gives greater emphasis to the therapeutic relationship as a core condition for therapy than the existential-humanistic one. Indeed, many existential-humanistic therapies elevate the role of this relationship from that of providing the conditions for therapy to that of providing the *means* of therapy. Epitomizing this position is the person-centred approach, a position encapsulated by the statement that it is the relationship which provides the 'necessary and sufficient conditions' for therapeutic change (Rogers 1957).

However, as R.H. indicates, not all existential-humanistic therapies share this view. Some consider the therapeutic relationship 'necessary' but not necessarily 'sufficient' (see Greenberg 1983). Others consider it, at times, neither 'sufficient' nor 'necessary' (see Perls 1969, 1973; Mahrer 1986, 1997). It is upon this striking diversity of attitudes and upon the rationales that give rise to them that I should like to focus. In doing so, I hope to suggest a paradox; namely, that the development of therapeutic diversity within the existential-humanistic school also signals the development of integration, particularly with regard to emerging attitudes to the therapeutic relationship. This paradoxical process can be usefully explored by considering two pioneering therapies – humanistically aligned, person-centred therapy and existentially aligned, gestalt therapy – together with their respective progenies.

Person-centred therapy

Person-centred therapists distinguish between self and self-concept (Mearns and Thorne 1988). The self is seen as real, unique, essentially trustworthy. The self-concept is a construct which, developing over years in response to the environment, is heavily dependent upon the attitudes of significant others. Usually, it is out of tune with the real self. In fact, the more conditional the love/'positive regard' that significant others offer – regard that is dependent upon the individual behaving in certain ways – the more conditioned and out of tune with the real self is the self-concept likely to be. For person-centred therapists, it is this 'out-of-tuneness' that causes psychological disturbance.

The self, however, never disappears and person-centred therapists, as R.H. suggests, start from the assumption that each individual, no matter how alienated from the self, has within them 'a self-actualizing tendency': 'the capacity . . . latent if not evident, to move forward toward maturity'. What is needed is a 'suitable psychological climate' for this 'tendency' to be 'released'. Released, the tendency 'becomes actual rather than potential' (Rogers 1961: 35).

For person-centred therapists, the 'suitable psychological climate' is encapsulated in the term 'core conditions'. These are conditions of 'empathy' (the capacity and willingness to enter the client's subjective perceptual world), 'congruence' (therapists' capacity to be in touch with their thoughts and feelings as they track those of their clients) and 'unconditional positive regard' (a respect for clients not for what they do or might be but for what they are) (Rogers 1957). Such conditions, sustained over time, not only offer an environment in which clients are freed from 'conditions of worth' (Rogers 1959) but a 'way of being' (Rogers 1980) which they can internalize. This 'way of being' takes on a transcendent note in Rogers' later writing, where he refers to the vibrant, sometimes 'strange', 'impulsive' spontaneity that marks a relaxed attunement to an 'inner, intuitive self': to the 'transcendental', 'unknown in me' (Rogers 1986b: 199). He refers to this attunement simply as 'presence', remarking that it alone proves 'releasing' both for himself and his clients. It is this 'mystical, spiritual dimension' that inspires some person-centred therapists to

invest even greater power in the transformative capacity of the therapeutic relationship (Thorne 1991, 1994).

Gestalt therapy
Gestalt therapy also assumes the existence of a 'self-actualizing'
tendency. This tendency is sustained by the capacity to creatively
adjust (Perls *et al.* 1951) – to stay 'open' to experience, to learn from
it and to make use of it to obtain what is needed. In turn, this capacity is dependent upon our versatility at forming gestalts: patterns of
perception that enable us to link aspects of ourselves and our situation, utilizing the 'contact boundary' (the point at which self and
other 'meet' and are potentially changed by that meeting) to seize
opportunities arising from such encounters.

The key to forming effective gestalts is 'awareness'. Without
awareness – of ourselves (sensations, emotions, thoughts, needs), of
our situation (in all its multifarious aspects) and of the potential
relationships between the two – the gestalts we form will be limited
and inadequate to the task of 'meeting' current needs. Furthermore,
we cannot simply rely on old gestalts formed from past experience,
since both we and our situations are in constant flux. 'Fixed gestalts',
particularly those formed in response to traumatic situations, narrow
our capacity to adjust creatively and limit our ability to 'self-actualize'.

Traditional gestalt therapy gives primacy to 'awareness' as 'curative factor' (Perls 1969). Any importance the relationship has is based
on its efficacy in achieving this end. For example, Perls (1969) suggests paying close attention to the relationship, since its qualities as
'an everchanging boundary where two people meet' (p. 6) can be
used to stimulate 'here-and-now' awareness. Its therapeutic usefulness rests upon the therapist's determination to play an active, even
manipulative role, doggedly refusing to engage in client games and
insisting on 'authenticity'. This insistence, which can be quite confrontational, is given far greater import than empathy, a therapeutic
condition that Perls (1973) warns against lest the therapist over-
identifies with the client and risks losing 'true contact'.

Traditional gestalt therapy's attitude to the role of the therapeutic
relationship can perhaps be understood by recognizing a premise,
not often explicit but probably inherited from Perls' psychoanalytic
background, that despite the individual's impulse to develop, there
appears to be a reluctance to do so. Indeed, speaking of clients he
remarks, 'I would say 90% don't go to a therapist to be cured, but to
get more adequate in their neurosis' (Perls 1969: 75). Furthermore,
as if echoing psychoanalysis's commitment to sustaining anxiety as

a necessary condition and motivating force of therapy, gestalt posits the concept of therapy as a 'safe emergency'. This oxymoron descriptively encapsulates a relational style in which support oscillates with provocation and where discovery and the re-mobilization of the individual's 'self-organizing' capacity is stimulated by means of 'skilful frustration' – a deliberate refusal to provide that which the client is seen as needing to provide him or herself.

Gestalt revisited

In practice, Perls' emphasis on therapist 'skill' becomes an emphasis on technical dexterity. Despite his disavowal of technique as 'gimmick', his preoccupation with it and on what could be 'done with' clients led to considerable criticism (see, for example, Perls' conversation with Friedman, in Friedman 1983). Not least has been the criticism that such an approach betrays the principle of authenticity, a principle that is consistent with the concept of I–Thou relating (Buber [1958] 1970; see R.H. above). Thus technique-oriented gestalt therapists have been accused of pursuing an I–It relationship in which the client becomes 'object' to be experimented upon (Greenberg 1983).

It was a reaffirmation of the principle of authenticity – a necessary condition, as Buber ([1958] 1970) suggests, for healing – that led many gestalt therapists to foreground the therapeutic relationship as determiner of techniques to be implemented (Yontef [1976] 1993), as focus of much of the therapeutic work (Polster and Polster 1973; Greenberg 1983) and even, perhaps, as the method of therapeutic cure. This marked shift is accompanied by a move away from the pursuit of awareness as primary therapeutic endeavour to the pursuit of 'contact'.[1]

'Contact' refers to the way an individual relates to his or her situation. Gestalt therapists identify a number of ways of relating that occur at the 'contact boundary' (see R.H. above). Relational flexibility (a willingness, where appropriate, to be open to, influenced by, even lost in that which we meet, alongside a capacity to resist surrender, to refuse to be moved or swayed) is seen as a marker of psychological health, just as the lack of flexibility (the tendency to relate in an habitual fashion) is seen as a marker of disturbance. Gestalt therapists argue that an authentic I–Thou relationship – one based on 'dialogue' (Hycner 1985; Jacobs 1989; Yontef 1993) in which therapist and client meet as persons and not as roles (Hycner 1991) – provides the context in which contact boundary disturbances can be noted by the therapist, brought to the awareness of the client and, through experimentation, changed.

A shift, too, seems evident in the attitude towards 'support'. Enabling 'self-support' (inner strength) has always been a goal of gestalt therapy. For example, 'skilful frustration' – the process of resisting clients' attempts to elicit therapist support – has long been a key technique for mobilizing clients' own self-supporting capacities. However, increasing interest in certain psychodynamic perspectives on early development, in particular the importance of empathy in meeting narcissistic needs (Tobin 1982; Jacobs 1992), has led to a revitalized emphasis on gestalt's core belief that we live and grow 'in relationship'.

In gestalt terms, a lack of 'support' (e.g. parental failure to 'meet' a child's needs) causes 'ruptures' in the relational field. This prompts in the child the experience, at best of being 'at odds' with the situation, at worst of deep exposure, humiliation, 'shame' (Wheeler 1995). Adapting to 'loss of support', the child calculates a 'frozen phenomenological formula' (Resnick and Parlett 1995): a 'fixed gestalt' which protects them from further shaming experiences but does so at the expense of spontaneity. Consequently, gestalt therapists attentive to the effect of such traumatizing experiences emphasize 'skilful support' more than 'skilful frustration', arguing that it is the supportive relationship that proffers the necessary safety without which no risk can be taken and no 'emergency' explored.

For those therapists whose focus is contact and whose practice foregrounds support, the I–Thou relationship may be viewed not only as a precondition for therapy but the measure of therapeutic success. Indeed, it might be argued that focusing on contact styles, eliciting awareness and experimenting simply serve to develop this relationship, and that it is the relationship that is fundamentally healing (Latner 1995).

Process-experiential therapy
For Rogers (1961), an essential measurement of therapeutic success is the client's relinquishment of rigid self-concepts and an emerging willingness to be a 'process of becoming'. Trusting in the organism, client and therapist 'float' in 'a complex stream of experience' (Rogers 1961: 153) – an existential description of the condition of congruence, now mutually proffered. This emphasis on the process of experiencing has led some humanistically oriented therapists to supplement the person-centred approach with techniques aimed at stimulating and intensifying the experiential process. R.H. alludes, for example, to focusing (Gendlin 1981). More radical have been the directive techniques advocated by process-experiential therapists (e.g. Greenberg

et al. 1993; Greenberg and Elliott 1997). It is not the purpose here to describe these techniques, merely to highlight that, in the context of these therapies, the core conditions proffered by therapeutic relationship, although still deemed 'necessary', are no longer deemed 'sufficient'. Indeed, although empathy is still given primacy, it is no longer described simply as a condition. Rather, it is a communicative activity specifically targeted at client affect and/or cognition in such a way as to aid the 'construction of self experience'.

The condition of empathy also plays a crucial role in Mahrer's (1986) experiential therapy – to such an extent that, in the pursuit of experiencing, he advocates complete identification with the client. This identification he calls 'alignment', a condition in which the therapist thinks, feels, sees what the client does and the therapeutic relationship is 'all but washed away' (Mahrer 1997). Such merger is intended to enhance the client's 'reliving' of experience to process it properly. This is set in contrast to 'relating' the experience to the therapist, an approach in which, Mahrer suggests, the relationship at best distracts, at worst intrudes.

The primacy given to experiential processing and the accompanying relegation of the relationship curiously echoes traditional gestalt therapy's fidelity to the 'royal road' of awareness. Indeed, both Mahrer's experiential therapy and Perlsian gestalt therapy promote practice in which the core conditions inherent in the therapeutic relationship may be seen to be neither sufficient nor, in fact, strictly necessary.

CHAPTER 5

Therapeutic environments: a comparative review

RICHARD HAZLER and NICK BARWICK

Introduction

Both research and clinical practice demonstrate that therapy works across theoretical approaches. Sometimes it works better than others; sometimes not at all. Psychodynamic, behavioural, cognitive-behavioural, humanistic and existential therapists, all experience success and failure. Even so, most practitioners tend to claim therapeutic superiority, insisting that their unique view of human beings and their specialized techniques for helping them constitute 'the right way'. However, as adamant as these claims might be, the mass of research and practice information tells us that, despite striking differences between approaches, there must be some critical factors in common for each approach to arrive at such similar results from such diverse starting points.

This book began with personalized reflections on how the differences that separate us (R.H. and N.B.) and the core facilitative factors/conditions that productively bind us can be compared to similar differences and bindings between therapeutic approaches and between therapist and client. In each of the three core chapters, we have focused on the internal points of difference and binding within each of the three broad theoretical frameworks: psychodynamic, cognitive-behavioural and existential-humanistic. Now, in this concluding chapter, we return to the original personalized model, comparing each of our conclusions about the common core facilitative conditions that we see as being recognizable across therapies. As we each respond in a way that is inevitably informed by our own particular theoretical, cultural and personal perspectives, we attempt to place the many fragments of information into a more generalized and more unified whole. Our aim here is not to reach finality or thorough summary but rather, through *our* dialogue, representing as it does individualized conclusions based on diverse points of view, to encourage a larger dialogue among readers. In this way, this chapter may provide an apt culmination to a joint project intended not only to proffer information and outline current views but, perhaps more importantly, to stimulate a continuing search by others for answers to the overriding question posited at the beginning of this book:

> *What conditions hold client and therapist together in productive ways when so many factors promote the downfall of the relationship?*

Core conditions

Involvement

R.H. Freud had clients recline on a couch in a position where he could not be seen. Perls sometimes stood, facing clients directly so that they could view him, touch him and talk about the sensations surrounding their physical and emotional interactions. Most modern therapists choose a middle ground by sitting, facing clients and discussing some combination of ideas, feelings, spirituality and/or behaviours. Now, at the beginning of the twenty-first century, more radical therapeutic connection models call for therapists to work over the telephone or even via the Internet with no actual physical proximity. These radical differences in how therapists connect with clients also underscore the essential importance of providing core facilitative conditions that create involvement and connection.

All therapy models demand involvement of client with therapist for therapy to progress. The only question remains, what kind and extent of involvement is essential? A degree of *honesty* on the parts of client and therapist seems to be one key general ingredient necessary to maintaining connection to the reality of the client's problems and to the realities of the therapeutic relationship. Honesty, in turn, requires some degree of *genuineness* from participants under the assumption that honesty as opposed to deception is attached to the actual person's beliefs. *Understanding* and *attachment* begin to emerge as this honest and genuine involvement promotes learning about the realities of the relationship and creates a sense of confident togetherness between therapist and client. Perhaps it is the place where the term 'therapeutic alliance' begins to take form.

Humanists may believe that this relationship is the core to all of therapy. Behaviourists may think it is mostly a necessary initial step in getting to the true work of therapy. Most theories and therapists find themselves somewhere in between these two extremes. There may be great discussion about the extent of impact that involvement has on therapy outcomes, but research and practice evidence clearly point to the necessity of creating a facilitative environment where some sufficient degree of involvement between client and therapist is mandatory.

N.B. Involvement describes the nature of a relationship: in individual therapy, the relationship between therapist and client and between both these and the work. Therapist involvement in the work – more importantly, perceived therapist involvement – provides an essential model for the client's own involvement in this respect. Mutual involvement is fundamental to establishing a working alliance and it is the working alliance which is now seen by most therapies as essential for maintenance of treatment.

Therapist and client involvement with each other, however, is an aspect of the alliance that is less universally accepted. Here, 'involvement' aptly describes the intimacies and intricacies of the therapeutic relationship. Empathic therapists step into their clients' worlds. Clients allow them to do so. Similarly, clients frequently 'get under the skin' of their therapists, whether their therapists wish them to or not. This inter-penetration can give rise to an intimate and intricate knowing. Yet to be involved is also to be entangled in trouble, difficulties – to be perplexed (see *Oxford English Dictionary*). Thus the therapeutic value of stepping into the inner life of another is only realized if one can step out again. Humanists refer to this as maintaining the 'as if' aspect of the condition of empathy. Psychodynamic therapists refer to it as 'counter-transference restraint'. Others talk of 'not playing the game' or 'resisting patient pull'. All are forms of personal involvement tempered by 'reserve'.

All this suggests that there is more agreement on this issue than there actually is. Differences can be usefully highlighted by identifying four groups. First are those therapies (traditional behavioural and cognitive-behavioural) that see personal involvement as neither necessary nor sufficient. Indeed, they suggest, it may even be unhelpful. Second, there are those (most contemporary cognitive-behavioural therapies) that see it as necessary although not sufficient – a *precondition* of therapy. Third, there are those (most post-rational cognitive-behavioural, most psychodynamic and those more actively oriented existential-humanistic therapies, e.g. Perlsian gestalt) that see it as an *essential condition*, in that it is a key source of and focus for the therapeutic work. Fourth, there are those (some post-rational cognitive-behavioural, some psychodynamic and those more non-directive existential-humanistic therapies, e.g. person-centred) that see it as a *transformative condition* that is both necessary and often sufficient for facilitating change.

For group one therapies, the less involved the therapist, the better. These therapies offer numerous clinical examples where there is no direct human contact at all; for example, bibliotherapy, tape-recorded instruction, downloads from the worldwide web. Indeed, too much contact, they argue, hinders generalization, since the therapist becomes the discriminative stimulus for behaviour change.

Group two's attitude is best captured in the concept of empirical collaboration: the relational condition in which therapy most effectively happens. This denotes a civil, rational, professional involvement, the purpose of which is to advance the scientific rigour of the work.

Group three gives primacy to a personal involvement that goes beyond the rational. It encourages inter-penetrative emotional involvement as a source of material for therapeutic work. When affect arising from this inter-penetration aids rather than impedes exploration, such involvement may be embraced in the concept of therapeutic alliance. When it leads to entanglement, however, the terms 'therapeutic misalliance' or 'alliance rupture' are more apt. In this event, therapist reserve is crucial; not a reserve that coldly rejects but one that refuses to be swallowed up or overwhelmed. Furthermore, the therapist must, at some point, be able to dialogue with a mature, rational, observing aspect of the client, capable of getting a purchase on what is happening rather than just experiencing it.

In the last group, experiencing is paramount and, potentially, the emotional involvement of both therapist and client is at its most unrestrained. In an effort to eschew the I–It relationship and to source the healing power of the I–Thou, mutual self-disclosure is not infrequent and therapist involvement with client more akin to another definition of this term: 'to enwrap . . . to enfold, envelop' (*Oxford English Dictionary*). For example, by providing an environment rich in the core condition of empathy, person-centred therapists seek to facilitate clients' own self-actualizing tendency. There is a link here with the psychodynamic notion of harnessing the client's developmental potential by offering a corrective emotional experience. This link is drawn upon in Mahrer's experiential therapy, where, in pursuit of that experience, therapist involvement with client is so great and identification so strong, distinctness gives way to merger.

Order

R.H. Clients come to counselling because their lives and thinking are in some form of disorder and confusion. Something is not as it should be or as clients would have it be. They come to therapy seeking ways to find purposeful means to create a more agreeable sense of their lives and actions. One key client task, then, is to find more productive order in their lives.

All therapeutic environments recognize the need for productive order as a core condition from the first client contact to the last. Therapists set times, places, fees and conditions for therapy to begin and to continue. Clients are provided with descriptions of how they will work together, what will go on in therapy and the kind of results that can be expected. Procedures described, what is emphasized and how much flexibility is available will differ across therapeutic orientations, but each one will provide the necessary order for their unique brand of therapy to proceed in the most productive way.

Robert Fancher (1995), in his book, *Cultures of Healing*, makes a strong case that forms of order are the most important facilitative condition of therapy. He demonstrates how all therapists and other forms of healers create a culture for clients in which they can feel sufficiently safe and confident that by sticking with the therapist-designed culture they will improve. It matters less whether this created culture is rigidly data-driven (as in behavioural therapy), highly formalized learning (as in transactional analysis) or allows great flexibility and informality (as in person-centred therapy). Whether the therapeutic culture focuses on the past, present or future is also not the key. What seems to be most important is that clients believe in the culturally ordered process provided by the therapist and are confident that following that process will lead them to a better life.

It is important to note that order can be productive or unproductive in a therapeutic environment just as it can be in life beyond therapy. Unproductive order is that which causes a clinging to thoughts, emotions or behaviours that have outlived their usefulness in the context of therapy. Productive order provides both clear direction and also flexibility to meet changes in the client, therapist or other factors in client environments. Therapists, therefore, take more control and provide more order early in therapy to guide the process, which is as yet relatively unknown to the client. Less order is provided later as clients gain understanding of the process and revise it to meet their changing therapeutic and life situations.

Individual growth and changing environments ensure that aspects of useful order must sooner or later become outdated and unproductive. The chaos resulting from previously productive order that has become unproductive demands creative changes to meet emerging conditions. The press of these chaotic points are natural parts of therapy that move therapist and client to search for new ways of revising the order in their environment. These creative adaptations are the ones that would not be considered as long as the individuals view environmental order in a single rigid way.

N.B. It is difficult to consider order without its opposite. Order brings relief yet 'Chaos gives birth to a dancing star' (Nietzsche [1895] 1972). Most therapies might agree with the first statement; Nietzsche's some might find eccentric.

As R.H. suggests, each therapeutic model offers a cohesive approach which is itself emblematic of order. This, together with the precision of boundaries (time, place, duration, etc.) may assure the client that personal chaos might yet be controlled. Nonetheless, again as R.H. implies, following initial relief, clients may soon find that some therapies deal, frustratingly, as much in further inducing chaos as in attempting to control it.

The highly ordered experimental conditions of behaviour therapy appear to offer most immediate relief to the anxieties of a disordered life. Clients are taught to restructure their approach to debilitating and chaos-inducing situations so the uncontrollable becomes controllable and the unmanageable becomes manageable. Cognitive-behavioural therapy, in its rational, structured, agenda-driven approach offers similar relief. Yet, paradoxically, cognitive-behavioural therapists also pursue an apparently antithetical course – de-construction. Since client problems are seen as resulting from irrational beliefs/schemata/personal constructs/personal rules of living, and so on, these require dismantling if clients are to relinquish rigid and deleterious patterns of thought. In effect, chaos needs inducing and enduring before new, more rational order can be born.

Piagetian therapists talk in terms of accommodation versus assimilation (Piaget 1952). The former describes the process by which acquisition of new information leads to an adjustment to, or change of, an existing belief. Since our early beliefs – inevitably based as they are on limited views of the world – constantly need revision, accommodation equates with healthy adaptation and growth. In contrast, assimilation is the process by which new information is integrated into powerful pre-existing beliefs. Our tendency is to assimilate rather than accommodate because change in core beliefs threatens identity – the way we order our concept of self around our beliefs. However, the energy needed to maintain the *status quo* in the face of new information taxes our rigid sense of order to breaking point – or to 'breakdown'.

'Breakdown' as a painful opportunity/condition for growth is an idea that is not uncommon among post-rational cognitive-behavioural, psychodynamic and existential-humanistic therapies. Although it is an idea that all too easily romanticizes a profoundly disturbing psychological state, it does pinpoint a belief, shared by these therapies, that client problems have their source in rigid and repressive patterns of thinking, feeling and behaving and that lasting relief lies in freedom from such repressive rigidity. These patterns, originally formed to protect the individual from real or imagined abandonment and feared disintegration lead, in the end, to an impoverished life and a narrowing and deadening of the capacity to experience.

It is the re-enlivening of clients' experiential capacity that the above therapies pursue. For them, the containing order of the therapeutic frame is so important because the chaos and conflict experienced within it is so great. 'Free association', 'going with the flow' or 'with what the client presents' do eventually offer order, but the process of finding it can feel chaotic. For this reason, clients pressure therapists into giving relief, be it in the form of premature interpretations, verbal or physical consolation, tasks or advice. Yet the aim of such therapy is to promote clients' capacity to tolerate the anxiety of 'not knowing', to embrace the fluidity of 'becoming' and, rather than relying on old 'schemata' or 'fixed gestalts', discover their own capacity to find order: to generate their own narratives, to creatively adapt/adjust, to contain.

Experimentation

R.H. Therapists bring theories and techniques to the counselling process that have been shown to work in some cases and to have failed in others. Clients arrive wanting something to be different in their existence, but not knowing exactly what it is or how to achieve it. An imperfect process, fallible participants and a desire to move towards some as yet unknown changes requires that both therapist and client be willing to experiment in the therapeutic environment. This is the condition needed for order and chaos to seek a productive level of interaction. Here is where the therapist and client must commit to the process of exploring potential ideas, options, experiences and then testing them against possible interpretations and outcomes.

The nature, content and aggressiveness in approach to experimentation in therapy are what differentiate theories from one another. Some emphasize the thinking or emoting aspect of experimentation, whereas others focus on behaviours. Testing internal perceptions gains the focus of some theories, while others attend more closely to external experience and the perceptions of others. Although the behaviourists and now the cognitive-behaviourists may most closely align themselves with the environment of experimental design and testing, all therapies require clients to choose, explore, test and re-evaluate based on the results of their experiments with change.

Therapy and client change require coming into contact with the unknowns of therapy progression, the development of the client–therapist relationship and the impact of new learning on life outside of therapy. Each participant must be prepared to test old and new feelings, conceptions and actions, recognize failed or inadequate ones and modify succeeding process steps based on what was learned from the core facilitative condition of experimentation.

N.B. Therapy is an experiment in living. As with any experiment, its purpose is to discover something as yet unknown. Such a discovery is paramount, since what is known or at least thought to be known has, as R.H. remarks, proved inadequate to the task of living. In the experiment that is therapy, some schools assign markedly unequal roles. In traditional behaviour therapy, for example, as in Perlsian gestalt or early psychoanalysis, the therapist is cast as experimenter, the client as experimented upon. Historically, however, the shift has been towards a more collaborative venture.

Accompanying this shift in roles has been a gradual shift in what is considered to be therapeutic about experimentation. Experimental products – insight, well-adapted behaviour, rational thought – arising from the therapist's work upon the client are still prized, yet perhaps more prized is a client's own experimental capacity. For some therapies (contemporary behavioural, rational cognitive-behavioural), this capacity is measured by client mastery of scientific procedure, evidence for which lies in the ability to utilize methods learnt in therapy to deal with the experiences of everyday life. For others (most post-rational cognitive-behavioural, existential-humanistic, psychodynamic), it is measured by the client's psychic agility: an openness to experiential flux and a willingness to 'play'.

Whichever process – scientific or experiential – is most prized, there is much similarity between therapies concerning those conditions deemed most suitable for promoting a client's capacity for experimentation. Perhaps most important among these is the therapist's genuine interest and judgemental restraint. These emerge in varying guises across therapies: unconditional positive regard, benevolent neutrality, evenly suspended attention, negative capability, hypothetical mindset, credulous approach. Yet all, as R.H. points out, encourage clients to try something different, to test out, to think, to play. Furthermore, these conditions, first offered by the therapist are, over time, imbibed by clients, better enabling them to sustain their own innate curiosity: their own experimental, indeed epistemological drive.

Trust

R.H. Trust is an unsaid word in the previous dialogues, which actually permeates all of them. Being involved, accepting new order and risking experimentation, each require a level of trust in the process and the participants. It is not a simple matter of client trusting therapist. The therapist must also trust clients to accept the process and their responsibilities within it. The collaborative nature of therapy requires a level of confidence in oneself, the other person and the process as a whole sufficient to allow other core conditions to be maintained.

Complete trust is an unreasonable ideal just as most ideals are impractical. Doubts and fears are normal parts of psychological warning systems, just as pain is necessary for our physical warning system. Touching a hot burner on the stove warns us to show a little caution when using the stove. Similarly, psychological fears and doubts call our attention to potential life hazards, the presence of which should cause us to consider adjusting our thoughts or actions. The result is that human beings are always in a process of building trust as opportunities for acquiescing to or overcoming fears and doubts make themselves continuously available in therapy and in life.

Person-centred therapists base their trust squarely on their belief in the human desire to develop in positive ways. More radical cognitive-behaviourists find their trust in the client's ability to think rationally and learn from environmental influences. Psychodynamic practitioners find their faith in the ability of clients to comprehend and then act on the complex interactions between internal mechanisms and the external world. Whatever the origins of their trust, however, all therapists must carry a level of trust in clients and the process if they are to proceed with therapy ethically.

Therapists' extensive training and experience serve to strengthen their basic trust in clients and the process even in the face of normal human fears and doubts. Clients do not have such training or experience to help deal with their normal fears and doubts, which are intensified during troubled times. So while therapists can bring a reasonably high level of trust to therapy, clients need to have their trust confirmed and expanded for therapy to be adequately facilitated.

N.B. Trust in oneself, each other and the process are, as R.H. outlines, conditions that facilitate all therapy. Indeed, without them in some degree, it is difficult to see how therapy could proceed at all. However, although all therapies agree on the need for trust, the nature of the different forms of trust and the therapeutic weight given to them varies from therapy to therapy.

Client trust in the process and the therapist is, again as R.H. suggests, a core condition in all therapies and fundamental to the working alliance. Thus, evidence of client mistrust may be viewed as evidence of an alliance rupture. Such ruptures manifest themselves in client anti-therapeutic behaviour, often called 'reactance' or 'resistance'.

These two terms say much not only about the source of client mistrust in therapist and process, but about the nature of the therapist's trust in the client. Reactance, for example (a term favoured by behavioural and most cognitive-behavioural therapists), describes a client's non-compliant, anti-therapeutic *reaction* to something the therapist has said or done. In effect, when a client does not comply with treatment, the fault – the source of mistrust – is seen as lying with the therapist and/or technique. This allocation of blame reveals its converse: a fundamental trust in the client's natural capacity to respond positively to treatment so long as that treatment is properly tailored, delivered and explained. Such a credo is embraced by most therapies other than mainstream psychodynamic therapy. Thus, in response to reactance and its accompanying alliance rupture, most behavioural therapists seek to modify technique. Social behaviour therapists, on the other hand, might modify delivery, adjusting the power-base to match client resource needs, whereas rational cognitive-behaviourists might aim, with varying degrees of persuasion, to proffer more convincing clarification of therapeutic rationale.

This implied trust in a client's openness and desire to change, so long as the therapeutic conditions are right, gathers even greater vitality in the humanist tradition. Here, the concept of the self-actualizing tendency evokes an essential optimism echoed also in certain psychodynamic schools (e.g. aspects of self-psychology). Both are informed by a belief in the existence of a healthy developmental drive, arrested only by environmental failure. Thus, although past experience of conditional prizing (or parental failure to meet narcissistic needs) may well stunt such development, therapists of these schools assert that it only requires the right (core) conditions for revitalization to occur. Many psychodynamic therapies, however, are not so trusting of client desire to change. They believe that the source of treatment non-compliance may lie as much in the client as in the failure of therapist or technique. To borrow a phrase from transactional analysis, there may be certain 'pay-offs' to be had from being unwell. It is this internally driven, usually unconscious refusal to change that the term 'resistance' describes.

For example, a young woman is eager to leave the parental home and go to university. Yet she is fearful that, if she does, the fragile parental relationship will finally fall apart. Fortuitously, she develops agoraphobia, thus enforcing home study and a concerned, united parental front. In therapy, such a patient may be less willing to change than her voluntary attendance at therapy, her agreement to carry out a tailored programme of treatment and her apparent understanding of treatment rationale might suggest. The irony lies, however, in the fact that, although resistance may impede therapeutic momentum, its existence offers clues as to which areas need most work. A similar view is held by post-rational cognitive therapists, who see resistance as inevitably arising from perceived threats to core schemata. Thus, paradoxically, resistance as a form of client mistrust is a condition which, if properly handled, can actually facilitate the therapeutic work.

The difference between therapies is perhaps most striking on the subject of the therapist's own trust in self. For behavioural and most cognitive-behavioural therapists, this trust is founded upon sound technical training and competent theoretical grasp. It is thus a professional form of trust and, as such, may inspire confidence and therapeutic compliance in the client undergoing treatment. For those therapies (psychodynamic, post-rational cognitive-behavioural and existential-humanistic) whose focus is the relationship itself, therapist trust in self is far more complex, more personal and more far-reaching in its potential effect on clients. This is because, for these therapies, the therapist is the instrument of therapy. Thus, therapists' capacity both to involve themselves in clients' worlds and to extricate themselves from that involvement is vital. Such a capacity is only possible if, to some considerable extent, therapists both know and can tolerate the nature of their own minds. This is why a core part of therapeutic training is the therapist's own therapy. In existential-humanistic training, this is strongly encouraged; in psychodynamic training, it is mandatory (see Jacobs and Rowan, forthcoming).

This aspect of training reveals an apprenticeship model. From a psychodynamic perspective, it is a model based on the primary apprenticeship – of infant to mother. Over time, trainee therapists experience: the intimate involvement arising from empathic attunement; the firm, reliable, safe holding derived from therapeutic order; the non-invasive, non-judgemental invitation to experiment and play. These experiences help establish trust, just as trust helps trainees to be open to these experiences. The result is a gradual relinquishment of rigid patterns of thought, feeling and behaviour, a greater capacity to tolerate ambivalence, to contain anxieties and to enter and 'float' in the 'complex stream of experience'. This essential trust in the self is the nature of congruence: a condition of mind the infectious quality of which acts as both vessel and agent of the therapeutic work.

Immediacy

R.H. Immediacy is the concept that defines the need for therapist and client to work together in the current time and present relationship. This present time is where the therapist has the greatest potential for seeking, recognizing and making use of potentially available information. Different therapies utilize the past and future in a wide variety of ways, but they all bring that information into the immediacy of the present situation with clients in order to make it useful.

The tremendous weight that existential-humanists place on the relationship between client and therapist gives the immediacy concept maximum importance. Many of the most powerful interactions are seen as those in which the content and feelings involved relate directly to the immediate situation between client and therapist. It is in this circumstance that feelings, thoughts, actions and words can be examined most directly. Therapists do not need to rely on whether clients are interpreting the actions of someone outside therapy accurately because they can see it first-hand. Clients do not need to guess at what the therapist's reactions to anxiety-ridden revelations will be, since they have full opportunity to hear, see and act upon those reactions directly.

Cognitive-behaviourists might not imbue the concept of immediacy with the wide-ranging impact given by existential-humanists, but they do make extensive use of it in understanding the client, goal-setting, decision-making and perhaps, most uniquely, in challenging client thinking and decision-making. It is in the immediacy of the situation where therapist challenges to client irrational thinking gain their strength. There is no time or space for discounting or avoiding the therapist's data-driven logic. The facts must be faced in the immediacy of the situation, whereas they could be manipulated or discounted in reference to the past or future.

A common perception of psychodynamic therapists and psychoanalysts is that they focus their efforts on the past rather than the present. This is relatively true compared with other theoretical orientations, but the concept obscures the importance these orientations also place on immediacy. The various forms of information collected in relation to the past or the unconscious are all impacted by a variety of techniques to bring them into the present time-frame. Dreams and free associations serve as classic examples of how information from outside the immediate interactions is brought into the immediate therapeutic environment. Once brought to the present, other techniques such as fostering and interpreting the transference are used to make the information an integral part of the immediate relationship between client and therapist.

N.B. Immediacy conceptualizes the therapeutic opportunity to experiment with the relationship between client and therapist in the 'here-and-now'. This is in line with the historical shift in therapeutic stance (from scientific detachment to inter-personal involvement) and in therapeutic focus (from experimental product – what made us who we are and what might make us different – to experimental process – how we are from moment-to-moment). What were once considered intrusions into the therapeutic experiment (by traditional behaviourism and early psychoanalysis, for example) are now widely perceived as providing useful opportunities for therapeutic intervention. In-session behaviour, script enactment, transference, client incongruence, all provide opportunities to work with core client issues in a live/'hot' way.

Strengthening the case for the therapeutic import of immediacy has been research into the vital role of emotion as well as cognition in the process of learning (see Greenberg and Safran 1989; Safran

1998). Immediacy is an environmental condition that engages both. Yet if immediacy offers the greatest opportunity for such engagement, the intense discomfort that can often characterize its presence means that it also runs the greatest risk of client and therapist disengaging altogether. What makes the difference – whether engagement or disengagement is more likely – is the condition of trust. A recognition of this has meant a burgeoning of literature, and of methods of review and assessment, focusing on ways of monitoring the therapeutic relationship and, where and when necessary, addressing and repairing the therapeutic alliance. This kind of attention, in unformalized fashion, has long been the staple diet of psychodynamic and, in particular, humanistic therapies, but is now common to behavioural and cognitive-behavioural therapies in more formalized and measurable ways.

The difference between most contemporary therapies, then, is not about whether they value immediacy but what they value it for. Some therapies (contemporary behavioural and rational cognitive-behavioural) value it as a useful condition (even precondition) which intensifies technical efficacy and consolidates learning. Others (most psychodynamic and some more actively oriented forms of existential-humanistic) value it as an essential condition in that it is a key source of therapeutic content. Still others (some post-rational cognitive-behavioural, some psychodynamic and some more non-directive humanistic therapies, e.g. person-centred) confer greatest value upon it, viewing it as a transformative condition; one which, in itself, is therapeutic. To borrow and blend a number of terms from existential, humanistic and psychodynamic therapies, immediacy well managed has the potential to offer the kind of empathic true contact in which the very containing and congruent presence of a non-judgemental therapist becomes a necessary and sufficient condition for therapeutic change.

Final thoughts: the cyclical nature of the facilitative environment

We began this book with an illustrative discussion of our co-authorial trials and the need for core environmental conditions to facilitate our progress towards a productive ending. It seems only fitting, then, that we tie the end of the book together in similar fashion. So, how does a comparison of core facilitative conditions across therapies relate to other potentially productive or unproductive professional relationships of which our co-authorship might serve as an example?

Our *involvement* with each other began in enthusiastic and positive ways, as many professional relationships do, by quickly attempting to create logical *order* out of the initial disorder and chaos of starting a major new project and relationship from scratch. As we *experimented* with and within this newly created *order*, it became clear that our efforts were not bringing mutually satisfying results, and intense feelings of frustration with ourselves, each other and the whole process were soon rife. Eventually, each of us managed to translate our thoughts and emotions into words, where the *immediacy* of potential failure created enormous additional demand for our direct professional attention. Fortunately, there was sufficient initial *trust* in ourselves and the process to struggle forward with continued *involvement* and *experimentation* rather than succumbing to the sense of relief that quitting seemed to hold. And so we continued *experimenting* with new creative forms of *order* in our working relationship and in the design and style of the book, even as we each longed and lobbied for the safe havens of our individual models, which had previously proven themselves for us as individuals.

Periodically, a new, mutually acceptable *order* formed that pushed us forward for a time, only to be called into question again as our conceptualizations and realizations of both the project and ourselves evolved. It became clear that the process of seeking *involvement*, creating *order*, *experimenting* with and within that order, emphasizing the *immediacy* of emerging thoughts, emotions and actions, and maintaining *trust* in ourselves and the process was not a simple set of steps that led to a single goal. Rather, these conditions constituted a recurring cycle of interactions that continually pushed us towards creative adaptation.

From a systemic point of view, however, even this cyclical description over-simplifies the struggle we underwent and the nature of the facilitative conditions that held us to task and to each other. At times, for example, so threatened was our *working alliance*, that it was not any particular aspect of our relationship or our work that bound us but our relationships with significant others: friends, family, senior editor.[1] This is an important environmental aspect to mention and one which we have not had time or space to explore within the confines of this book. It is an aspect, however, that is essential for the therapist to take into account before embarking on work with a client. Does the client have a stable enough social network outside therapy to sustain them between sessions and, if not, how might the therapeutic approach be modified to meet this very real client need? Furthermore, what is the context in which the therapist is working? Is there sufficient supervisory, organizational and personal support, or are concerns at these various levels of interaction so disturbing that the therapist has insufficient 'self-support' let alone the capacity to support the painful explorations of another. Despite a tendency among both therapists and authors to see the difference between success and failure residing in the conditions which those directly involved in the work create, this is an overly precious and omnipotent view. The reality is that the facilitative conditions necessary for creative and effective exploration to occur live not only in the dyadic work-relationship, but in the relational systems in which each of the main participants is imbedded.

In the end, thanks to the conditions that we have struggled to create and maintain and those that we have been fortunate enough to draw upon, we have created a book that we can both accept as a credible combination of ourselves at this point in time. Of course, in doing so, we must learn to bear certain disappointments, certain losses. Each relationship and what it gives birth to must carry with it the recognition that what it is, is not what it might have been. Yet the mark of a facilitative relationship is that what it is and what it gives birth to can be celebrated as 'good enough'.

Our scenario, then, is not dissimilar to that experienced by therapist and client, although complicated by the fact that, as co-authors, we each play therapist and client to each other, at different and sometimes awkward times. Both scenarios involve the struggle to create and maintain a facilitative environment: an environment in which each participant can hope to make 'good enough' use of their skills, abilities, knowledge and actions. In large part, the measure of the efficacy of this environment lies in the condition of the relationship that emerges between participants. It is, after all, through the productive therapeutic relationship that clients (and perhaps therapists) grow towards more adaptive interactions with their changing real-life environments, and it is through the relationship that each participant, be they therapeutic or authorial, gains hope of discovering more than either might have discovered alone.

Notes

Introduction

1 Unless otherwise indicated, 'therapy' refers to *individual* psychotherapy (as opposed to couple, family or group) with *adults* (as opposed to adolescents or children). Although non-individual therapies have much in common with individual ones, they may also prompt further modifications in both approach and the conditions in which that approach is made. Within the confines of this book, there is insufficient room for such an elaboration.

The term 'therapist' describes the person offering therapy, be it clinical psychologist, analytical psychologist, psychoanalyst, psychotherapist or counsellor. Similarly, although for the most part we use the term 'client' to describe the person undergoing therapy, in certain contexts the term 'patient' is employed instead. Again, these terms are interchangeable; however, as with their counterparts, they say something important about the philosophies, psychological paradigms and core conditions encouraged by the different therapeutic schools. For example, the term 'psychotherapist' or 'psychoanalyst' is more often coupled with the term 'patient', whereas 'client' is more often coupled with the term 'counsellor'. The former pairing is, to some extent, associated with the view of a specialist doing something to a person who is sick, while the latter invests greater power in the receiver of therapy, casting them in the role of purchaser of services. For some, the counsellor–client nomenclature more adequately describes the collaborative nature of therapy and aptly purges the relationship of connotations of authoritarian reductionism. For others, however, it suggests an unrealistic degree of control and composure on the part of the person coming for therapy. Reminding us that 'patient' is rooted in the Latin *pati* (to suffer), it is the psychotherapist–patient nomenclature, some argue, that tells it how it is.

Chapter 1

1 Clinical material provided by N.B.

Chapter 2

1 Kleinian object relations theory does not sit in either category easily. Since its theoretical base is instinct-driven, it is in accord with the drive-discharge paradigm. Yet its clinical practice elevates the therapeutic relationship, if not to curative factor, then to primary source of therapeutic material. In this, its affinity is with the relational paradigm. Interpersonalists (e.g. Sullivan, Fromm, Horney, etc.) are also often, somewhat problematically, embraced by this nomenclature.
2 For an interesting article on the importance of the therapist's love, see Gerrard (1996).
3 The frame offers therapists safety too (Levenson 1992). Its predetermined boundaries hold them in a way that parallels the way they seek to hold patients, and offer a second blank screen to carry some of the projective weight.
4 Issues of power are central to feminist-informed psychodynamic approaches, since egalitarianism and shared power represent the ideal relationship. Openly discussing the power relationship between therapist and patient/client, as well as disclosing therapist values, orientation and technique are some of the ways that some feminist therapists seek to promote an egalitarian environment and divest themselves and their profession of mystery (Eichenbaum and Orbach 1983).
5 Franklin (1990) comments on how patients' rage and destructiveness can be sealed off by therapists' detachment and suggests that interactional assistance may offer some liberation to such patients as well as patients who are inhibited by fears of intimate relatedness.
6 An important and unfortunate irony needs to be highlighted here when discussing the egalitarian perspective advocated by Jung, since, in his effort to attribute fixed characteristics to specific nations, his writing contains anti-Semitic and nationalistic ideas that are anything but egalitarian. For an exposition of the socio-political issues, see Samuels (1993).
7 The use of the chair is now common among many psychodynamic therapies if working with patients on a once-weekly basis.
8 Jung ([1954] 1966) advocates a rejection of any predetermined 'shoulds' of therapy and encourages the therapist's adaptation to the individual patient.
9 For a clear elucidation of these complex, core Lacanian concepts, see, for example, Fink (1999) or Evans (1996).
10 Lacan uses the German 'Es' (Freud's word) rather than 'Id' (Strachey's translation of Freud) to highlight the pun on 'S' for Subject/Sujet. For a clear and brief exposition of the significance of this pun, see relevant entries in Evans (1996).

11 Again, for elucidation of this core concept – 'the Other' – see Evans (1996).

12 Lacanians refer to their patients as 'analysands'. They favour this term as it places the activity of analysis/therapy firmly in the hands of the individuals seeking it (something the word 'patient' does not do) without feeding the delusion that they are master of their problem or of the process they are about to embark upon (something the word 'client' does).

13 For some intriguing accounts – both positive and negative – of patient responses to this idiosyncratic disruption of the therapeutic environment, see Schneiderman (1983), Anzieu (1986, cited in Oliner 1998) and Fink (1999).

14 The striking resemblance to Jung and Fordham's phrase, 'organ of information' (see above), is clear. Fordham (1957) refers to the therapist's 'syntonic countertransference'. This concept sheds its pathological connotations in his later work in the term 'interactional dialectic' (1979).

15 So too does the frame (Langs 1974; Quinodoz 1992).

16 Jung remarked, 'Learn your theories. Then, when the patient walks through the door, forget them' (cited in Stevens 1994: 102).

17 Bion draws here on a term coined by Keats which the poet uses in a letter to George and Thomas Keats (21 December 1817) when describing the creative capacities which writers such as Shakespeare appeared to possess.

18 This is in keeping with Jung's (1956) view that therapy should support regression (see also Maduro and Wheelwright 1977).

19 See also Bollas' (1989) 'destiny drive'.

20 Building upon the notion of the holding environment and its primary import in the therapeutic environment when dealing with 'resourceless' patients, Khan (1983, 1988) developed a form of 'analytic care' more authoritative than Winnicott's, more fatherly than motherly. Consequently, it has been referred to as 'managing' rather than 'holding' (see Cooper 1993).

21 My thanks to Ellen Noonan for bringing this aspect of a patient's use of the therapist to my attention.

22 For a comparative link between Kohut's view of transference and Jung's (i.e. as a dynamic interaction that is purposeful and requires authentic response rather than analysis), see Jacoby (1981, 1984).

23 Greenson (1971) sees the working alliance receding in the final phase of therapy, giving way to a full-blown real relationship.

24 Malan (1992) sees Freud as having taken a wrong turn in reacting to 'increasing resistance with increased passivity'.

25 He draws here on a paper by Bonaparte (1940).

26 Mann draws on Rank's ([1929] 1973) concept of the birth trauma, the first experience of separation and individuation.

27 It is perhaps salutary to remember that the grandfather of psychodynamic therapy, whose strict recommendations began this chapter, evinced in his practice a 'flexibility' that would shock the psychodynamic sensibilities of most contemporary psychodynamic therapists, from whatever school (see Malcolm [1981] 1988; Gay 1988).

Chapter 3

1 For a useful summary of these and other views, see Gelso and Hayes (1998).
2 For a comprehensive review of this literature, see Schaap *et al.* (1993).
3 Wryly, this has been called the 'doctrine of immaculate perception'. For a fuller account of philosophical differences between rational and post-rational cognitive-behavioural therapies, see Mahoney and Lyddon (1988) and Neimeyer (1993).
4 This concept clearly draws on the humanistic tradition (see Chapter 4).

Chapter 4

1 For a full discussion of these two views and their impact on the role of the relationship, see Hycner and Jacobs (1995).

Chapter 5

1 A useful analogy may be made between our authorial selves as a 'couple' on the one hand and the senior editor as 'couple therapist' on the other.

References

Abram, J. (1996) *The Language of Winnicott: A Dictionary of Winnicott's Use of Words*. London: Karnac Books.

Adler, G. (1966) *Studies in Analytical Psychology*. London: Hodder & Stoughton.

Adler, G. (1985) *Borderline Psychopathology and its Treatment*. New York: Jason Aronson.

Ainsworth, M. (1982) Attachment: Retrospect and prospect, in C.M. Parkes and J. Stevenson-Hinde (eds) *The Place of Attachment in Human Behaviour*. London: Tavistock.

Alexander, F. and French, T. (1946) *Psychoanalytic Therapy: Principles and Applications*. New York: Ronald Press.

Alexander, J.F., Barton, C., Schiavo, R.S. and Parsons, B.V. (1976) Systems behavioural intervention with families of delinquents: Therapist characteristics, family behaviour, and outcome, *Journal of Consulting and Clinical Psychology*, 44: 656–64.

Allyon, T. and Michael, J. (1959) The psychiatric nurse as a behavioral engineer, *Journal of the Experimental Analysis of Behavior*, 2: 323–34.

Angus, L.E. and Rennie, D.L. (1989) Envisioning the representational world: The client's experience of metaphoric expression in psychotherapy, *Psychotherapy*, 26: 372–9.

Anzieu, D. (1975) *L'auto-analyse de Freud et la découverte de la psychoanalyse*. Paris: Presses Universitaires de France.

Bacal, H.A. and Newman, K. (1990) *Theories of Object Relations: Bridges to Self Psychology*. New York: Columbia University Press.

Balint, M. ([1965] 1985) *Primary Love and Psycho-Analytic Technique*. London: Karnac Books.

Balint, M. ([1968] 1989) *The Basic Fault*. London: Routledge.

Balint, M. (1986) The unobtrusive analyst, in G. Kohon (ed.) *The British School of Psychoanalysis: The Independent Tradition*. London: Free Association Books.

Bandura, A. (1965) Vicarious processes: A case of no-trial learning, in L. Berkowits (ed.) *Advances in Experimental Social Psychology*, Vol. 2. New York: Academic Press.

Bandura, A. (1969) *Principles of Behaviour Modification*. New York: Holt, Rinehart & Winston.

Bandura, A. (1971) Vicarious and self-reinforcement processes, in R. Glaser (ed.) *The nature of reinforcement*. New York: Academic Press.

Bandura, A. (1977) *Social Learning Theory*. Englewood Cliffs, NJ: Prentice-Hall.

Beck, A.T. (1979) *Cognitive Therapy and the Emotional Disorders*. New York: International Universities Press.

Beck, A.T. and Weishaar, M.E. (1995) Cognitive therapy, in R.J. Corsini and D. Wedding (eds) *Current Psychotherapies*, 5th edn. Itasca, IL: Peacock.

Beck, A.T., Freeman, A.F. and Associates (1990) *Cognitive Therapy of Personality Disorders*. New York: Guilford Press.

Beck, A.T., Wright, F.D., Newman, C.F. and Liese, B.S. (1993) *Cognitive Therapy of Substance Abuse*. New York: Guilford Press.

Benjamin, J. (1994) What angel would hear me? The erotics of transference, *International Journal of Psychoanalysis*, 41: 535–57.

Bennet, E.A. (1982) *Meetings with Jung*. London: Anchor Press.

Beutler, L.E., Machado, P.P. and Neufeldt, S.A. (1994) Therapist variables, in A. Bergin and S. Garfield (eds) *Handbook of Psychotherapy and Behavior Change*, 4th edn. New York: Wiley.

Binswanger, L. (1963) *Being-in-the-World: Selected Papers of Ludwig Binswanger* (J. Needleman, trans.). New York: Basic Books.

Bion, W. ([1959] 1984) Attacks on linking, in *Second Thoughts*. London: Karnac Books.

Bion, W. ([1962] 1984) A theory of thinking, in *Second Thoughts*. London: Karnac Books.

Bion, W. ([1967] 1988) Notes on memory and desire, in E.B. Spillius (ed.) *Melanie Klein Today: Vol. 2: Mainly Practice*. London: Routledge.

Bion, W. ([1970] 1984) *Attention and Interpretation*. London: Karnac Books.

Bion, W. ([1974] 1990) *Brazilian Lectures*. London: Karnac Books.

Bleger, J. (1967) Psychoanalysis of the psychoanalytic frame, *International Journal of Psycho-Analysis*, 48: 513–19.

Blum, H.P. (1981) Some current and recurrent problems of psychoanalytic technique, *Journal of the American Psychoanalytic Association*, 21: 61–76.

Bohart, A.C. and Greenberg, L.S. (1997) *Empathy Reconsidered*. Washington, DC: American Psychological Association.

Bollas, C. (1989) *Forces of Destiny*. London: Free Association Books.

Bollas, C. (1990) The origins of the therapeutic alliance, *Paper presented to a Weekend Conference for English-speaking Members of European Societies*, London.

Bonaparte, M. (1940) Time and the unconscious, *International Journal of Psycho-Analysis*, 21: 427–68.

Bordin, E.S. (1979) The generalizability of the psychoanalytic concept of the working alliance, *Psychotherapy: Theory, Research and Practice*, 16: 252–60.

Boss, M. (1963) *Psychoanalysis and daseinsanalysis* (L.B. Lefebre, trans.). New York: Basic Books.

Bower, T. (1977) *A Primer of Infant Development*. San Francisco, CA: Freeman.

Bowlby, J. ([1969] 1982) *Attachment*, Vol. 1, 2nd edn. Harmondsworth: Penguin Books.

Bowlby, J. (1988) *A Secure Base: Clinical Applications of Attachment Theory*. London: Routledge.

Brazelton, T. and Cramer, B. (1991) *The Earliest Relationship*. London: Karnac.

Brenner, C. (1979) Working alliance, therapeutic alliance and transference, *Journal of the American Psychoanalytic Association*, 27 (suppl.): 137–57.

Buber, M. ([1958] 1970) *I and Thou*. New York: Charles Scribner's Sons.

Bugental, J.F.T. (1965) *The Search for Authenticity*. New York: Holt, Rinehart & Winston.

Bugental, J.F.T. (1978) *Psychotherapy and Process*. Reading, MA: Addison Wesley.

Bugental, J.F.T. (1987) Aristophanes, William, Rollo May, and our dog Dickens, *Humanistic Psychologist*, 24: 221–30.

Bugental, J.F.T. and Sterling, M.M. (1995) Existential-humanistic psychotherapy: New perspectives, in A.S. Gurman and S.B. Messer (eds) *Essential Psychotherapies*. New York: Guilford Press.

Burns, D.D. and Auerbach, A. (1996) Therapeutic empathy in cognitive-behavioural therapy: Does it really make a difference?, in P.M. Sakoviskis (ed.) *Frontiers of cognitive therapy*. New York: Guilford Press.

Casement, P.J. ([1982] 1986) Some pressures on the analyst for physical contact, in G. Kohon (ed.) *The British School of Psychoanalysis: The Independent Tradition*. London: Free Association Books.

Casement, P.J. ([1985] 1990) *On Learning from the Patient*. London: Routledge.

Chused, J.F. and Raphling, D.L. (1992) The analyst's mistakes, *Journal of the American Psychoanalytic Association*, 40: 89–116.

Clarkson, P. (1995) *The Therapeutic Relationship*. London: Whurr Publishers.

Coltart, N. (1986) Slouching towards Bethlehem, in G. Kohon (ed.) *The British School of Psychoanalysis: The Independent Tradition*. London: Free Association Books.

Coltart, N. (1992) *Slouching Towards Bethlehem*. London: Free Association Books.

Coltart, N. (1996) The self: What is it?, in V. Richards and G. Wilce (eds) *The Person Who is Me: Contemporary Perspectives on the True and False Self*. London: Karnac/The Squiggle Foundation.

Consumer Reports (1995) Mental health: Does therapy work?, *Consumer Reports*, 60: 734–9.

Cooper, J. (1993) Different ways of structuring the frame: According to Winnicott, Khan and Langs, *Journal of the British Association of Psychotherapists*, 24: 23–35.

Coren, A. (1996) Brief therapy – base metal or pure gold?, *Psychodynamic Counselling*, 2(1): 22–38.

Cormier, W.H. and Cormier, L.S. (1991) *Interviewing Strategies for Helpers: Fundamental Skills and Cognitive Behavioral Interventions*, 3rd edn. Pacific Grove, CA: Brooks/Cole.

Craighead, L.W., Craighead, W.E., Kazdin, A.E. and Mahoney, M.J. (1994) *Cognitive and Behavioural Interventions: An Empirical Approach to Mental Health Problems*. Boston, MA: Allyn & Bacon.

Davanloo, H. (ed.) (1978) *Basic Principles and Techniques in Short Term Dynamic Psychotherapy*. New York: Spectrum.

Davanloo, H. ([1980] 1993) *Short-term Dynamic Psychotherapy*. New York: Jason Aronson.

Dember, W.N. (1974) Motivation and the cognitive revolution. *American Psychologist*, 29(3): 161–8.

Dorn, F.J. (1986) *The Social Influence Process in Counseling and Psychotherapy.* Springfield, IL: Thomas.

Dupont, J. (ed.) (1988) *The Clinical Diary of Sandor Ferenczi.* Cambridge, MA: Harvard University Press.

Eagle, M.N. and Wolitzky, D.L. (1997) Empathy: a psychoanalytic perspective, in A.C. Bohart and L.S. Greenberg (eds) *Empathy Reconsidered: New Directions in Psychotherapy.* Washington DC: American Psychological Association.

Ehrenberg, D.B. (1984) Pychoanalytic engagement, II: Affective considerations, *Contemporary Psychoanalysis,* 20: 560–83.

Ehrenberg, D.B. (1992) *The Intimate Edge.* New York: W.W. Norton.

Eichenbaum, L. and Orbach, S. (1983) *Understanding Women: A Feminist Psychoanalytic Approach.* New York: Basic Books.

Eigen, M. (1980) On the significance of the face, *Psycho-Analytic Review.*

Eissler, K.R. (1953) The effect of the structure of the ego on psychoanalytic technique, *Journal of the American Psychoanalytic Association,* 1: 104–43.

Elliott, J.M. (1999) Feminist theory, in D. Capuzzi and D.R. Gross (eds) *Counseling & Psychotherapy,* 2nd edn. Columbus, OH: Merrill.

Ellis, A. (1962) *Reason and Emotion in Psychotherapy.* New York: Lyle Stuart.

Ellis, A. (1995) Rational-emotive therapy, in R.J. Corsini and D. Wedding (eds) *Current Psychotherapies,* 5th edn. Itasca, IL: Peacock.

Ellis, A. and Dryden, W. (1997) *The Practice of Rational Emotive Behavior.* New York: Springer.

Elson, M. (ed.) (1987) *The Kohut Seminars on Self Psychology and Psychotherapy with Adolescents and Young Adults.* New York: W.W. Norton.

Epstein, M. (1996) *Thoughts Without a Thinker.* London: Duckworth.

Erikson, E. ([1950] 1981) *Childhood and Society.* London: Paladin.

Evans, D. (1996) *Dictionary of Lacanian Psychoanalysis.* London: Routledge.

Evans, R. (1976) Development of the treatment alliance in the analysis of an adolescent boy, *The Psychoanalytic Study of the Child,* 31: 193–224.

Eysenck, H.J. (1960) *Behaviour Therapy and the Neuroses.* Oxford: Pergamon Press.

Fairbairn, W.R.D. (1952) *Psycho-Analytic Studies of the Personality.* London: Tavistock.

Fancher, R. (1995) *Cultures of Healing.* New York: W.H. Freeman.

Fenichel, O. (1941) *Problems of Psychoanalytic Technique.* New York: Psychoanalytic Quarterly.

Ferenczi, S. ([1928] 1980) The elasticity of psycho-analytic technique, in M. Balint (ed.) *Final Contributions to the Problems and Methods of Psycho-Analysis* (E. Mosbacher and others, trans.). London: Maresfield.

Ferenczi, S. ([1930] 1980) The principles of relaxation and neocatharsis, in M. Balint (ed.) *Final Contributions to the Problems and Methods of Psycho-Analysis* (E. Mosbacher and others, trans.). London: Maresfield.

Ferenczi, S. ([1932] 1980) The analyst's attitude to his patient, in M. Balint (ed.) *Final Contributions to the Problems and Methods of Psycho-Analysis* (E. Mosbacher and others, trans.). London: Maresfield.

Fink, B. (1999) *A Clinical Introduction to Lacanian Psychoanalysis: Theory and Technique.* Cambridge, MA: Harvard University Press.

Fliess, R. (1942) The metapsychology of the analyst, *Psychoanalytic Quarterly,* 11: 211–27.

Foa, E.B. and Foa, U.G. (1980) Resource theory: Interpersonal behavior as exchange, in K.J. Gergen, M.S. Greenberg and R.J. Willis (eds) *Social Exchange: Advances in Theory and Research*. New York: Plenum Press.

Fonagy, P. (1990) Discussion of C. Bollas's paper, 'The Origins of the Therapeutic Alliance', *Paper presented to a Weekend Conference for English-speaking Members of European Societies*, London.

Fordham, M. (1957) *New Developments in Analytical Psychology*. London: Routledge & Kegan Paul.

Fordham, M. ([1960] 1974) Countertransference, in M. Fordham (ed.) *Technique in Jungian Analysis*. London: Heinemann.

Fordham, M. (1979) Analytical psychology and countertransference, in L. Epstein and A. Feiner (eds) *Countertransference*. New York: Jason Aronson.

Fox, R.P. (1984) The principle of abstinence reconsidered, *International Review of Psychoanalysis*, 2: 227–36.

Frank, J.D. and Frank, J.B. (1991) *Persuasion and Healing*, 3rd edn. Baltimore, MD: Johns Hopkins University Press.

Frank, M.L. (1999) Existential theory, in D. Capuzzi and D.R. Gross (eds) *Counseling and Psychotherapy: Theories and Interventions*, 3rd edn. Upper Saddle River, NJ: Prentice-Hall.

Frankl, V.E. (1963) *Man's Search for Meaning: An Introduction to Logotherapy*. Boston, MA: Beacon Press.

Frankl, V.E. (1997) *Victor Frankl Recollections: An Autobiography*. New York: Insight Books/Plenum Press.

Franklin, G. (1990) The multiple meanings of neutrality, *Journal of the American Psycho-Analytic Association*, 38: 195–220.

Freud, A. ([1936] 1992) *The Ego and the Mechanisms of Defence*. London: Karnac.

Freud, S. ([1900/1914] 1976) *The Interpretation of Dreams*, Pelican Freud Library, Vol. 4. Harmondsworth: Pelican.

Freud, S. ([1910] 1959) The future prospects of psycho-analytic therapy, *Standard Edition of the Complete Psychological Works of Sigmund Freud*, Vol. 20. London: Hogarth Press.

Freud, S. ([1912a] 1958) Recommendations to physicians practising psychoanalysis, *Standard Edition of the Complete Psychological Works of Sigmund Freud*, Vol. 12. London: Hogarth Press.

Freud, S. ([1912b] 1958) The dynamics of transference, *Standard Edition of the Complete Psychological Works of Sigmund Freud*, Vol. 12. London: Hogarth Press.

Freud, S. ([1913] 1958) On beginning the treatment (further recommendations on the technique of psycho-analysis), *Standard Edition of the Complete Psychological Works of Sigmund Freud*, Vol. 12. London: Hogarth Press.

Freud, S. ([1914] 1958) Remembering, repeating and working through, *Standard Edition of the Complete Psychological Works of Sigmund Freud*, Vol. 12. London: Hogarth Press.

Freud, S. ([1915] 1958) Observations on transference love, *Standard Edition of the Complete Psychological Works of Sigmund Freud*, Vol. 12. London: Hogarth Press.

Freud, S. ([1916–17] 1991) *Introductory Lectures on Psychoanalysis*, Penguin Freud Library, Vol. 1. Harmondsworth: Penguin.

Freud, S. ([1919] 1955) Lines of advance in psycho-analytic theory, *Standard Edition of the Complete Psychological Works of Sigmund Freud*, Vol. 17. London: Hogarth Press.

Freud, S. ([1920] 1991) Beyond the Pleasure Principle, *On Metapsychology*, Penguin Freud Library, 11. Harmondsworth: Penguin.

Freud, S. ([1923a] 1991) The ego and the id, *On Metapsychology*, Penguin Freud Library, Vol. 11. Harmondsworth: Penguin.

Freud, S. ([1923b] 1955) Two encyclopaedia articles, *Standard Edition of the Complete Psychological Works of Sigmund Freud*, Vol. 18. London: Hogarth Press.

Freud, S. ([1937] 1964) Analysis terminable and interminable, *Standard Edition of the Complete Psychological Works of Sigmund Freud*, Vol. 23. London: Hogarth Press.

Freud, S. ([1940] 1993) An outline of psychoanalysis, *Psychoanalysis: Its History and Development*, Penguin Freud Library, Vol. 15. Harmondsworth: Penguin.

Freud, S. and Breuer, J. ([1895] 1991) The case of Anna O, *Studies on Hysteria*, Penguin Freud Library, Vol. 3. Harmondsworth: Penguin.

Friedman, L. (1986) Kohut's testament, *Psychoanalytic Inquiry*, 6: 321–47.

Friedman, M. (1983) *The Healing Dialogue in Psychotherapy*. New York: Jason Aronson.

Fromm, E. (1941) *Escape from Freedom*. New York: Holt, Rinehart & Winston.

Fromm, E. (1947) *Man for Himself*. New York: Holt, Rinehart & Winston.

Galassi, J.P. and Perot, A.R. (1992) What you should know about behavioural assessment, *Journal of Counselling and Development*, 70: 624–31.

Garfield, S.L. and Bergin, A.E. (1994) Introduction and historical overview, in A. Bergin and S. Garfield (eds) *Handbook of Psychotherapy and Behavior Change*, 4th edn. New York: Wiley.

Gay, P. (1988) *Freud: A Life of Our Times*. New York: W.W. Norton.

Gelso, C.J. and Carter, J.A. (1985) The relationship in counseling and psychotherapy: Components, consequences and theoretical antecedents, *The Counseling Psychologist*, 13: 155–243.

Gelso, C.J. and Hayes, J.A. (1998) *The Psychotherapy Relationship: Theory, Research, and Practice*. New York: Wiley.

Gendlin, E.T. (1962) *Experiencing and the Creation of Meaning*. New York: Free Press.

Gendlin, E.T. (1981) *Focusing*. New York: Bantam Books.

Gendlin, E.T. (1996) *Focusing-oriented Psychotherapy: A Manual of the Experiential Method*. New York: Guilford Press.

Gerrard, J. (1996) Love in the time of psychotherapy, *British Journal of Psychotherapy*, 13(2): 163–73.

Gill, M.M. (1982a) *Analysis of Transference*, Vol. 1. New York: International Universities Press.

Gill, M.M. (1982b) The point of view of psychoanalysis: Energy discharge or person?, *Psychoanalysis and Contemporary Thought*, 4: 523–51.

Gill, M.M. (1988) The interpersonal paradigm and the degree of the therapist's involvement, in B. Wolstein (ed.) *Essential Papers on Countertransference*. New York: New York University Press.

Glasgow, R.E., Schafer, C. and O'Neill, H.K. (1981) Self help books and amount of therapist contact in smoking cessation programs, *Journal of Consulting and Clinical Psychology*, 49: 659–67.

Goldberg, A. (ed.) (1978) *The Psychology of the Self*. New York: International Universities Press.

Goldberg, A. (1988) *A Fresh Look at Psychoanalysis: The View from Self Psychology*. Hillsdale, NJ: Analytic Press.

Goodman, A. (1992) Empathy and inquiry: Integrating empathic mirroring in an interpersonal framework, *Contemporary Psychoanalysis*, 28: 631–46.

Grand, S., Rechetnick, J., Podrug, D. and Schwager, E. (1985) *Transference in Brief Psychotherapy*. Hillsdale, NJ: Analytic Press.

Grant, J. and Crawley, J. (forthcoming) *Transference and Mirrors to the Self*. Buckingham: Open University Press.

Greenacre, P. ([1968] 1971) The psychoanalytic process, transference and acting out, *Emotional Growth*. New York: International Universities Press.

Greenberg, L.S. (1983) The relationship in Gestalt therapy, in M.J. Lambert (ed.) *Psychotherapy and Patient Relationships*. Homewood, IL: Dow Jones-Irwin.

Greenberg, L.S. and Elliott, R. (1997) Varieties of empathic responding, in A.C. Bohart and L.S. Greenberg (eds) *Empathy Reconsidered: New Directions in Psychotherapy*. Washington, DC: American Psychological Association.

Greenberg, L.S. and Safran, J.D. (1989) Emotion in psychotherapy, *American Psychologist*, 44(1): 19–29.

Greenberg, L.S., Rice, L.N. and Elliott, R. (1993) *Process–Experiential Therapy: Facilitating Emotional Change*. New York: Guilford Press.

Greeno, B.P., Kolodinsky, R.W. and Sampson, J.P. (1997) Counseling on the information highway: The future possibilities and potential problems, *Journal of Counseling and Development*, 75: 203–12.

Greenson, R.R. (1958) Variations in classical psycho-analytic technique, *International Journal of Psychoanalysis*, 39: 200–1.

Greenson, R.R. (1965) The working alliance and the transference neurosis, *Psychoanalytic Quarterly*, 34: 155–81.

Greenson, R.R. (1967) *The Technique and Practice of Psycho-Analysis*. London: The Hogarth Press/Institute of Psychoanalysis.

Greenson, R.R. (1971) The 'real' relationship between the patient and the psychoanalyst, in M. Kanzer (ed.) *The Unconscious Today*. New York: International Universities Press.

Groesbeck, C. (1975) The archetypal image of the wounded healer, *Journal of Analytical Psychology*, 20(2): 122–45.

Grünbaum, A. (1984) *The Foundations of Psychoanalysis: A Philsosphical Critique*. Berkeley, CA: University of California Press.

Guggenbühl-Craig, A. (1971) *Power in the Helping Professions*. New York: Springer.

Guidano, V.F. (1991) *The Self in Process: Towards a Post-Rationalist Cognitive Therapy*. New York: Guilford Press.

Guidano, V.F. and Liotti, A.C. (1985) A constructivistic foundation for cognitive therapy, in M.J. Mahoney and A. Freeman (eds) *Cognition and Psychotherapy*. New York: Plenum Press.

Gutheil, T.G. and Havens, L.L. (1979) The therapeutic alliance: contemporary meanings and confusions, *International Review of Psycho-Analysis*, 6: 467–81.

Haak, N. (1957) Comments on the analytical situation, *International Journal of Psychoanalysis*, 38: 183–95.

Hani, A.G. (1973) The rediscovery of the therapeutic alliance, *International Journal of Psychoanalytic Psychotherapy*, 2: 449–77.

Hanly, C.M.T. (1994) Reflections on the place of the therapeutic alliance in psychoanalysis, *International Journal of Psychoanalysis*, 75: 457–67.

Hartmann, H. ([1939] 1958) *Ego Psychology and the Problem of Adaptation*. London: Imago.

Hazler, R.J. (1999) Person-centered theory, in D. Capuzzi and D.R. Gross (eds) *Counseling and Psychotherapy*, 2nd edn. Columbus, OH: Merrill.

Heidegger, M. (1962) *Being and Time*. New York: Harper & Row.

Heimann, P. (1950) On counter-transference, *International Journal of Psycho-Analysis*, 31: 81–4.

Heppner, P.P. and Claiborn, C.D. (1989) Social influence research in counseling: A review and critique, *Journal of Counseling Psychology*, 36: 365–87.

Hinshelwood, R.D. (1991) *A Dictionary of Kleinian Thought*. London: Free Association Books.

Hoffer, A. (1990) Review of 'The Clinical Diary of Sandor Ferenczi', *International Journal of Psychoanalysis*, 71: 723–7.

Holmes, J. (1992) *Between Art and Science*. London: Routledge.

Holmes, J. (1993) *John Bowlby and Attachment Theory*. London: Routledge.

Homans, G.L. ([1961] 1974) *Social Behavior: Its Elementary Forms*. New York: Harcourt Brace Jovanovich.

Horowitz, M.J. (1988) *Introduction to Psychodynamics: A New Synthesis*. Northvale, NJ: Jason Aronson.

Horvath, A.O. and Greenberg, L.S. (1994) Introduction, in A. Horvath and L. Greenberg (eds) *The Working Alliance: Theory, Research, and Practice*. New York: Wiley.

Horvath, A.O. and Symonds, B.D. (1991) Relation between working alliance and outcome in psychotherapy: A meta-analysis, *Journal of Counseling Psychology*, 38: 133–49.

Hunt, M. (1993) *The Story of Psychology*. New York: Doubleday.

Hycner, R. (1985) Dialogical Gestalt therapy: An initial proposal, *The Gestalt Journal*, 8(1): 23–49.

Hycner, R. (1991) *Between Person and Person: Toward a Dialogical Psychotherapy*. New York: Gestalt Journal Press.

Hycner, R. and Jacobs, L. (1995) *The Healing Relationship in Gestalt Therapy*. Highland, NY: Gestalt Journal Press.

Jacobs, L. (1989) Dialogue in Gestalt theory and therapy, *The Gestalt Journal*, 12(6): 25–67.

Jacobs, L. (1992) Insights from psychoanalytic self-psychology and inter-subjectivity theory for gestalt therapists, *The Gestalt Journal*, 15(2): 25–60.

Jacobs, M. and Rowan, J. (forthcoming) *The Therapist's Use of Self*. Buckingham: Open University Press.

Jacobs, T.J. (1991) *The Use of Self: Countertransference and Communication in the Analytic Situation*. Madison, CT: International Universities Press.

Jacobson, J.G. (1993) Developmental observation, multiple models of the mind, and the therapeutic relationship in psychoanalysis, *Psychoanalytic Quarterly*, 62: 523–52.

Jacobson, N.S. (1989) The therapist–client relationship in cognitive behavior therapy: Implications for treating depression, *Journal of Cognitive Psychotherapy*, 3: 85–96.

Jacoby, M. (1981) Reflections on H. Kohut's concept of narcissism, *Journal of Analytical Psychology*, 26(1): 19–32.

Jacoby, M. (1984) *The Analytic Encounter: Transference and Human Relationship*. New York: Inner City Books.

Janis, J.L. (1982) Helping relationships: A preliminary theoretical analysis, in I.L. Janis (ed.) *Counseling in Personal Decisions: Theory and Research on Short Term Helping Relationships*. New Haven, CT: Yale University Press.

Jaques, E. (1982) Review of 'The Work of Hanna Segal', *International Journal of Psycho-Analysis*, 63: 502–4.

Joseph, B. (1985) Transference – the total situation, *International Journal of Psycho-Analysis*, 66: 447–54.

Jung, C.G. ([1954] 1966) *The Collected Works of C.G. Jung, Vol. 16: The Practice of Psychotherapy* (H. Read, M. Fordham and G. Adler, eds; R.F.C. Hull, trans.). London: Routledge & Kegan Paul.

Jung, C.G. (1956) *The Collected Works of C.G. Jung, Vol. 5: Symbols of Transformation* (H. Read, M. Fordham and G. Adler, eds; R.F.C. Hull, trans.). London: Routledge & Kegan Paul.

Jung, C.G. ([1963] 1977) *Memories, Dreams, Reflections*. Glasgow: Collins, Fount Paperbacks.

Kalodner, C.R. (1995) Cognitive-behavioral theories, in D. Capuzzi and D.R. Gross (eds) *Counseling and Psychotherapy: Theories and Interventions*. Englewood Cliffs, NJ: Merrill.

Kanfer, F.H. (1996) Motivation and emotion in behaviour therapy, in K.S. Dobson and K.D. Craig (eds) *Advances in Cognitive-Behavioral Therapy*. Thousand Oaks, CA: Sage.

Karon, B.P. and VandenBos, G.R. (1981) *Psychotherapy of Schizophrenia*. New York: Jason Aronson.

Katz, J. (1985) The sociopolitical nature of counseling, *The Counseling Psychologist*, 13: 615–24.

Kelly, G.A. (1955) *The Psychology of Personal Constructs*. New York: W.W. Norton.

Kernberg, O. (1980) *Internal World and External Reality*. New York: Jason Aronson.

Khan, M.M.R. (1974) *The Privacy of Self*. London: Hogarth Press.

Khan, M.M.R. (1983) *Hidden Selves*. London: Hogarth Press.

Khan, M.M.R. (1988) *When Spring Comes*. London: Chatto & Windus.

Kierkegaard, S. (1944) *The Concept of Dread* (W. Lowrie, trans.). Princeton, NJ: Princeton University Press.

Klauber, J. (1986) Elements of the psychoanalytic relationship and their therapeutic implications, in G. Kohon (ed.) *The British School of Psychoanalysis: The Independent Tradition*. London: Free Association Books.

Klein, M. ([1952] 1988) The origins of transference, in *Envy & Gratitude and Other Works 1946–1963*. London: Virago.

Kohut, H. (1971) *The Analysis of the Self*. New York: International Universities Press.

Kohut, H. (1977) *The Restoration of the Self.* New York: International Universities Press.

Kohut, H. (1981) *Remarks on Empathy* (film). Filmed at a Conference on Self-Psychology, Los Angeles, 4 October.

Kohut, H. (1984) *How does Analysis Cure?* Chicago, IL: University of Chicago Press.

Kohut, H. and Wolf, E.S. (1978) The disorders of the self and their treatment: An outline, *International Journal of Psychoanalysis,* 59: 413–25.

Kottler, J.A. (1991) *The Complete Therapist.* San Francisco, CA: Jossey-Bass.

Kottler, J.A. and Hazler, R.J. (1997) *What You Never Learned in Graduate School: A Survival Guide for Therapists.* New York: W.W. Norton.

Kottler, J.A. and Hazler, R.J. (2001) Therapist as a model of humane values and humanistic behavior, in K.J. Schneider, J.F.T. Bugental and J.F. Pierson (eds) *The Handbook of Humanistic Psychology: Leading Edges in Theory, Research and Practice.* Thousand Oaks, CA: Sage.

Kottler, J.A., Sexton, T.L. and Whiston, S.C. (1994) *The Heart of Healing: Relationships in Therapy.* San Francisco, CA: Jossey-Bass.

Krasner, L. (1962) The therapist as a social reinforcement machine, in H.H. Strupp and L. Luborsky (eds) *Research in Psychotherapy.* Washington, DC: American Psychological Association.

Kron, R.E. (1971) Psychoanalytic complications of a narcissistic transference, *Journal of the American Psychoanalytic Association,* 19: 636–53.

Lacan, J. (1951) Some reflections on the ego, *International Journal of Psycho-Analysis,* 34: 11–17.

Lacan, J. ([1953] 1977) The function and field of speech and language in psychoanalysis, in *Ecrits: A Selection* (A. Sheridan, trans.). London: Tavistock Publications.

Lacan, J. ([1953–54] 1988) *The Seminar, Book 1: Freud's Papers on Technique* (J. Forrester, trans.). Cambridge: Cambridge University Press.

Lacan, J. ([1954–55] 1988) *The Seminar, Book 2: The Ego in Freud's Theory and in the Technique of Psychoanalysis* (S. Tomaselli, trans.). Cambridge: Cambridge University Press.

Lacan, J. ([1955–56] 1993) *The Seminar, Book 3: The Psychoses* (R. Grigg, trans.). London: Routledge.

Lacan, J. ([1960] 1977) The subversion of the subject and the dialectic of desire in the Freudian unconscious, in *Ecrits: A Selection* (A. Sheridan, trans.). London: Tavistock.

Lacan, J. ([1964] 1977) *The Seminar, Book 11: The Four Fundamental Concepts of Psychoanalysis* (A. Sheridan, trans.). London: Hogarth Press/Institute of Psychoanalysis.

Langs, R. (1974) *The Technique of Psychoanalytic Psychotherapy,* 2 Vols. New York: Jason Aronson.

Langs, R. (1975a) The therapeutic relationship and deviations in technique, *International Journal of Psychoanalytic Psychotherapy,* 4: 106–41.

Langs, R. (1975b) Therapeutic misalliances, *International Journal of Psychoanalytic Psychotherapy,* 4: 77–105.

Langs, R. (1976) *The Therapeutic Interaction,* 2 Vols. New York: Jason Aronson.

Langs, R. (1978) *Technique in Transition.* New York: Jason Aronson.

Langs, R. (1980) *Interactions: The Realm of Transference and Counter Transference.* New York: Jason Aronson.

Langs, R. (1988) The ground rules or frame of psychotherapy, in *A Primer of Psychotherapy.* New York: Gardner Press.

LaPlanche, J. and Pontalis, J.B. ([1973] 1988) *The Language of Psychoanalysis.* London: Karnac/Institute of Psychoanalysis.

Latner, J. (1995) Letter, *British Gestalt Journal*, 4(1): 49–50.

Lazarus, A.A. (1963) The results of behavior therapy in 126 cases of severe neurosis, *Behaviour Research and Therapy*, 1: 69–80.

Lazarus, A.A. (1995) Multi-modal therapy, in R.J. Corsini and D. Wedding (eds) *Current Psychotherapies*, 5th edn. Itasca, IL: Peacock.

Leitner, L.M. (1995) Optimal therapeutic distance: A therapist's experience of personal construct psychotherapy, in R.A. Neimeyer and M.J. Mahoney (eds) *Constructivism in Psychotherapy*. Washington, DC: American Psychological Association.

Levant, R.F. and Shlien, J.M. (eds) (1984) *Client Centered Therapy and the Person Centered Approach: New Directions in Theory, Research and Practice.* New York: Praeger.

Levenson, E. (1992) Mistakes, errors and oversights, *Contemporary Psychoanalysis*, 28: 555–71.

Lewin, B.D. (1955) Dream psychology and the analytic situation, *Psychoanalytic Quarterly*, 24: 169–99.

Linden, J.A. (1994) Gratification & provision in psychoanalysis: Should we get rid of the 'Rule of Abstinence'?, *Psychoanalytic Dialogues*, 4: 549–82.

Liotti, G. (1991) Patterns of attachment and the assessment of interpersonal schemata: Understanding and changing difficult patient–therapist relationships in cognitive psychotherapy, *Journal of Cognitive Psychotherapy* 5: 105–14.

Lipton, S.D. (1977) Clinical observations on resistance to the transference, *International Journal of Psycho-Analysis*, 58: 463–72.

Little, M. (1990) *Psychotic Anxieties and Containment: A Personal Record of an Analysis with Winnicott.* Northvale, NJ: Jason Aronson.

Loewenstein, R.M. (1972) Ego autonomy and psychoanalytic technique, *Psychoanalytic Quarterly*, 41: 1–22.

Lomas, P. (1987) *The Limits of Interpretation: What's Wrong with Psychoanalysis?* Harmondsworth: Pelican.

Luborsky, L. (1984) *Principles of Psychoanalytic Psychotherapy: A Manual for Supportive-Expressive Treatment.* New York: Basic Books.

Luborsky, L. (1994) Therapeutic alliances as predictors of psychotherapy outcomes: Factors explaining the predictive success, in A. Horvath and L. Greenberg (eds) *The Working Alliance: Theory, Research, and Practice.* New York: Wiley.

Luborsky, L. Crits-Christoph, P., Mintz, J. and Auerbach, A. (1988) *Who Will Benefit from Psychotherapy? Predicting Therapeutic Outcomes.* New York: Basic Books.

Lyddon, W.J. (1990) First- and Second-order change: Implications for rationalist and constructivist therapies, *Journal of Counseling and Development*, 69: 122–7.

Macalpine, I. (1950) The development of the transference, *Psychoanalytic Quarterly*, 19: 501–39.

Maddux, J.E., Stoltenberg, C.D. and Rosenwein, R. (eds) (1987) *Social Processes in Clinical and Counseling Psychology*. New York: Springer.

Maduro, R. and Wheelwright, J. (1977) Analytical psychology, in R. Corsini (ed.) *Current Personality Theories*. Itasca, IL: Peacock.

Mahler, M.S. (1968) *On Human Symbiosis and the Vicissitudes of Individuation*. New York: Basic Books.

Mahoney, M.J. (1991) *Human Change Processes: Notes on the Facilitation of Personal Development*. New York: Basic Books.

Mahoney, M.J. and Lyddon, W.J. (1988) Recent developments in cognitive approaches to counseling and psychotherapy, *The Counseling Psychologist*, 16(2): 190–234.

Mahrer, A.R. (1986) *Therapeutic Experiencing*. New York: W.W. Norton.

Mahrer, A.R. (1997) Empathy as therapist–client alignment, in A.C. Bohart and L.S. Greenberg (eds) *Empathy Reconsidered: New Directions in Psychotherapy*. Washington, DC: American Psychological Association.

Malan, D.H. (1976) *The Frontier of Brief Psychotherapy: An Example of the Convergence of Research and Clinical Practice*. New York: Plenum Press.

Malan, D.H. (1992) *Psychodynamics, Teaching and Outcome in Brief Psychotherapy*. London: Butterworth/Heinemann.

Malcolm, J. ([1981] 1988) *Psychoanalysis: The Impossible Profession*. London: Karnac Books.

Mann, J. (1973) *Time-Limited Therapy*. Cambridge, MA: Harvard University Press.

Maroda, K.J. (1991) *The Power of Countertransference*. Northvale, NJ: Jason Aronson.

Maslow, A.H. (1943) A theory of human motivation, *Psychological Review*, 50: 370–96.

Maslow, A.H. (1954) *Motivation and Personality*. New York: Harper & Row.

Maslow, A.H. (1968) *Toward a Psychology of Being*. New York: Van Nostrand Reinhold.

Masterson, J.F. (1976) *Psychotherapy of the Borderline Adult: A Developmental Approach*. New York: Brunner/Mazel.

Masterson, J.F. (1985) *The Real Self: A Developmental, Self and Object Relations Approach*. New York: Brunner/Mazel.

Masterson, J.F. and Klein, R. (eds) (1989) *Psychotherapy of the Disorders of the Self: The Masterson Approach*. New York: Brunner/Mazel.

May, R. (1953) *Man's Search for Himself*. New York: W.W. Norton.

May, R. (ed.) (1961) *Existential Psychology*. New York: Random House.

May, R. (1969) *Love and Will*. New York: W.W. Norton.

Mearns, D. and Thorne, B.J. (1988) *Person-Centred Counselling in Action*. London: Sage.

Mehlman, R.D. (1976) Transference mobilization, transference resolution and the narcissistic alliance. Paper presented to the Boston Psychoanalytic Society, 25 February.

Meichenbaum, D. (1985) *Stress Inoculation Training*. New York: Pergamon Press.

Meissner, W.W. (1996) *The Therapeutic Alliance*. New Haven, CT: Yale University Press.

Meltzer, D. (1968) *The Psycho-Analytic Process*. Perth: Clunie.

Menninger, R. (1958) *Theory of Psychoanalytic Technique*. New York: Basic Books.

Messer, S.B. and Warren, C.S. (1995) *Models of Brief Psychodynamic Therapy: A Comparative Approach*. New York: Guilford Press.

Meyer, V. and Bartlett, D. (1976) Behavior therapy: Technology or psychotherapy?, *Scandinavian Journal of Behavior Therapy*, 5: 1–12.

Miller, L.K. (1980) *Principles of Everyday Behavior Analysis*. Monterey, CA: Brooks/Cole.

Milner, M. (1952) Aspects of symbolism in comprehension of the not-self, *International Journal of Psychoanalysis*, 33: 181–95.

Mitchell, S. (1988) *Relational Concepts in Psychoanalysis*. Cambridge, MA: Harvard University Press.

Modell, A.H. (1976) 'The holding environment' and the therapeutic action of psychoanalysis, *Journal of the American Psychoanalytic Association*, 24: 285–307.

Monk, G., Winslade, J., Crocket, K. and Epston, D. (eds) (1997) *Narrative Therapy in Practice: The Archaeology of Hope*. San Francisco, CA: Jossey-Bass.

Moraitis, G. (ed.) (1995) The relevance of the couch in contemporary psychoanalysis, *Psychoanalytic Inquiry*, 15.

Morris, R.J. and Magrath, K.H. (1983) The therapeutic relationship in behavior therapy, in M.J. Lambert (ed.) *Psychotherapy and Patient Relationships*. Homewood, IL: Dow Jones-Irwin.

Morris, R.J. and Morris, Y.P. (1992) A behavioural approach to intervention, in R.C. D'Amato and B.A. Rothlisberg (eds) *Psychological Perspectives on Interventions*. New York: Longman.

Moss, D. (1985) What you see is what you get: Empiricism, psychoanalytic theory and brief therapy, *PsychCritique*, 1: 21–34.

Mowrer, O.H. (1964) Freudianism, behavior therapy and 'self-disclosure', *Behavior Research and Therapy*, 1: 321–31.

Neimeyer, R.A. (1993) An appraisal of constructivist therapy, *Journal of Consulting and Clinical Psychology*, 61: 221–34.

Neimeyer, R.A. (1995a) Client-generated narratives in psychotherapy, in R.A. Neimeyer and M.J. Mahoney (eds) *Constructivism in Psychotherapy*. Washington, DC: American Psychological Association.

Neimeyer, R.A. (1995b) Constructivist psychotherapies: Features, foundations and future directions, in R.A. Neimeyer and M.J. Mahoney (eds) *Constructivism in Psychotherapy*. Washington, DC: American Psychological Association.

Neimeyer, R.A. and Mahoney, M.J. (1995) *Constructivism in Psychotherapy*. Washington, DC: American Psychological Association.

Nietzsche, F. ([1895] 1972) *Thus Spake Zarathustra*, trans. R.J. Hollingdale. London: Penguin.

Novick, J. (1970) The vicissitudes of the 'working alliance' in the analysis of a latency girl, *The Psychoanalytic Study of the Child*, 25: 231–56.

Oliner, M. (1998) Jacques Lacan: The language of alienation, in P. Marcus and A. Rosenberg (eds) *Psychoanalytic Versions of the Human Condition: Philosophies of Life and their Impact on Practice*. New York: New York University Press.

Parham, T. (1996) M.C.T. theory and African–American populations, in D. Sue, A. Ivey and P. Pedersen (eds) *A Theory of Multicultural Counseling and Therapy*. Pacific Grove, CA: Brooks/Cole.

Parry, C.W. and Birkett, D. (1996) The working alliance: A re-appraisal, *British Journal of Psychotherapy*, 12(3): 291–9.

Pavlov, I.P. (1927) *Conditioned Reflexes* (W.H. Gantt, trans.). New York: International Publishers.

Pedder, J.R. ([1976] 1986) Attachment and new beginning: Some links between the work of Michael Balint and John Bowlby, in G. Kohon (ed.) *The British School of Psychoanalysis: The Independent Tradition*. London: Free Association Books.

Pedersen, P. (1994) *A Handbook for Developing Cultural Awareness*, 2nd edn. Alexandria, VA: American Counseling Association.

Perls, F. (1969) *Gestalt Therapy Verbatim*. Lafayette, CA: Real People Press.

Perls, F. (1973) *The Gestalt Approach*. Palo Alto, CA: Science & Behavior.

Perls, F. (1976) *The Gestalt Approach and Eye Witness to Therapy*. New York: Bantam.

Perls, F., Hefferline, R. and Goodman, P. (1951) *Gestalt Therapy: Excitement and Growth in the Human Personality*. New York: Julian Press.

Persons, J.B. and Burns, D.D. (1985) Mechanism of action of cognitive therapy: Relative contribution of technical and interpersonal intervention, *Cognitive Therapy and Research*, 9(5): 539–55.

Peterfreund, E. (1983) *The Process of Psychoanalytic Therapy: Models and Strategies*. Hillsdale, NJ: Analytic Press.

Peters, M. (1991) Analytic neutrality and the 'person' as psychoanalyst, *Psychoanalysis and Psychotherapy*, 9: 114–27.

Phillips, A. (1988) *Winnicott*. London: Fontana.

Piaget, J. (1952) *The Origin of Intelligence in the Child*. New York: International Universities Press.

Pine, F. (1990) *Drive, Ego, Object and Self: A Synthesis for Clinical Work*. New York: Basic Books.

Polster, E. and Polster, M. (1973) *Gestalt Therapy Integrated*. New York: Vintage Books.

Prouty, G. (1994) *Theoretical Evolutions in Person-Centered/Experiential Therapy*. London: Praeger.

Quinodoz, D. (1992) A psychoanalytic setting as the instrument of the container function, *International Journal of Psychoanalysis*, 73: 627–35.

Rabavilas, A.D., Boulougouris, J.C. and Perissaki, C. (1979) Therapists' qualities related to outcome with exposure *in vivo* in neurotic patients, *Journal of Behavior Therapy and Experimental Psychiatry*, 10: 293–9.

Rank, O. ([1929] 1973) *The Trauma of Birth*. New York: Harper & Row.

Raue, P.J. and Goldfried, M.R. (1994) The therapeutic alliance in cognitive-behavior therapy, in A.O. Horvath and L.S. Greenberg (eds) *The Working Alliance: Theory, Research and Practice*. New York: Wiley.

Renik, O. (1995) The ideal of the anonymous analyst and the problem of self-disclosure, *Psychoanalytic Quarterly*, 64: 466–95.

Resnick, R. and Parlett, N. (1995) Gestalt therapy: Principles, prisms and perspectives, *British Gestalt Journal*, 4(1): 3–13.

Robins, C.J. and Hayes, A.M. (1993) An appraisal of cognitive therapy, *Journal of Consulting and Clinical Psychology*, 61(2): 205–14.

Rogers, C.R. (1942) *Counseling and Psychotherapy*. Boston, MA: Houghton Mifflin.

Rogers, C.R. (1951) *Client-Centered Therapy*. Boston, MA: Houghton Mifflin.

Rogers, C.R. (1957) The necessary and sufficient conditions of therapeutic personality change, *Journal of Consulting Psychology*, 21: 95–103.

Rogers, C.R. (1959) A theory of therapy, personality, and interpersonal relationships, as developed in the client-centred framework, in S. Koch (ed.) *Psychology: A Study of Science: Vol. 3. Formulations of the Person and the Social Context*. New York: McGraw-Hill.

Rogers, C.R. (1961) *On Becoming a Person*. Boston, MA: Houghton Mifflin.

Rogers, C.R. (1977) *Carl Rogers on Personal Power*. New York: Delacorte Press.

Rogers, C.R. (1980) *A Way of Being*. Boston, MA: Houghton Mifflin.

Rogers, C.R. (1986a) Reflection of feelings, *Person-Centered Review*, 1: 375–7.

Rogers, C.R. (1986b) A client-centered/person-centered approach to therapy, in I. Koutash and A. Wolf (eds) *Psychotherapist's Casebook: Therapy and Technique in Practice*. San Francisco, CA: Jossey-Bass.

Rosenfeld, H. ([1987] 1990) *Impasse and Interpretation: Therapeutic and Anti-Therapeutic Factors in the Psychoanalytic Treatment of Psychotic, Borderline, and Neurotic Patients*. London: Routledge.

Russell, C. (1996) What is the difference between a 'psychoanalytic' and a so-called 'normal', everyday relationship? The controversy between Freud and Ferenczi, *British Journal of Psychotherapy*, 13(1): 37–52.

Safran, J.D. (1998) *Widening the Scope of Cognitive Therapy: The Therapeutic Relationship, Emotion and the Process of Change*. Northvale, NJ: Jason Aronson.

Safran, J.D. and Segal, Z.V. (1990) *Interpersonal Process in Cognitive Therapy*. New York: Basic Books.

Samuels, A. (1985) *Jung and the Post-Jungians*. London: Routledge & Kegan Paul.

Samuels, A. (1993) *The Political Psyche*. London: Routledge.

Samuels, A., Shorter, B. and Plaut, F. (1986) *A Critical Dictionary of Jungian Analysis*. London: Routledge.

Sandler, J. (1983) Reflections on some relations between psychoanalytic concepts and psychoanalytic practice, *International Journal of Psycho-Analysis*, 64: 35–45.

Sandler, J., Dare, C. and Holder, A. (1992) *The Patient and the Analyst*, revised and expanded by J. Sandler and U. Dreher. London: Karnac Books.

Schaap, C.P., Bennun, I., Schindler, L. and Hoogduin, K. (1993) *The Therapeutic Relationship in Behavioral Psychotherapy*. New York: Wiley.

Schachter, J. (1994) Abstinence and neutrality: Development and diverse views, *International Journal of Psychoanalysis*, 75: 709–20.

Schachter, J. (1995) The analyst under stress: Issues of technique, *Journal of the American Psychoanalytic Association*, 43: 11–14.

Schafer, R. ([1983] 1993) *The Analytic Attitude*. London: Karnac Books.

Schlesinger, H.J. (1994) How the analyst listens, *International Journal of Psychoanalysis*, 75: 31–7.

Schneiderman, S. (1983) *Jacques Lacan*. Cambridge, MA: Harvard University Press.

Segal, H. (1977) Countertransference, *International Journal of Psychoanalytic Psychotherapy*, 6: 31–7.

Segal, H. ([1981] 1986) *The Work of Hanna Segal: A Kleinian Approach to Clinical Practice*. London: Karnac Books.

Shapiro, T. (1974) The development and distortions of empathy, *Psychoanalytic Quarterly*, 43: 4–25.

Sifneos, P. (1987) *Short-Term Dynamic Therapy: Evaluation and Technique*, 2nd edn. New York: Plenum Press.

Skinner, B.F. (1938) *Behavior of Organisms*. New York: Appleton-Century-Crofts.

Skinner, B.F. (1953) *Science and Human Behavior*. New York: Macmillan.

Skinner, B.F. (1976) *Particulars of My Life*. New York: Knopf.

Smith, B. (ed.) (1988) *Foundations of Gestalt Therapy*. Hemsbach, Germany: Philosophia Verlag Munchen Wien.

Spitz, R.A. (1956) Transference: The analytical setting and its prototype, *International Journal of Psycho-Analysis*, 37: 380–5.

Sterba, R. (1934) The fate of the ego in psychoanalytic therapy, *International Journal of Psychoanalysis*, 15: 117–26.

Stern, D. (1985) *The Interpersonal World of the Infant*. New York: Basic Books.

Stevens, A. (1994) *Jung*. Oxford: Oxford University Press.

Stolorow, R.D. (1986) Critical reflections on the theory of self psychology: An inside view, *Psychoanalytic Inquiry*, 6: 387–402.

Stolorow, R.D., Brandchaft, B. and Atwood, G.E. (1987) *Psychoanalytic Treatment: An Intersubjective Approach*. Hillsdale, NJ: Analytic Press.

Stolorow, R.D., Brandchaft, B. and Atwood, G.E. (eds) (1994) *The Intersubjective Perspective*. Northvale, NJ: Jason Aronson.

Stone, L. (1961) *The Psychoanalytic Situation*. New York: International Universities Press.

Strong, S.R. and Claiborn, C.D. (1982) *Change Through Interaction*. New York: Wiley.

Strupp, H. (1973) Toward a reformulation of the psychotherapeutic influence, *International Journal of Psychiatry*, 11: 263–354.

Strupp, H.H. and Binder, J.L. (1984) *Psychotherapy in a New Key: A Guide to Time-Limited Dynamic Psychotherapy*. New York: Basic Books.

Sullivan, H.S. (1954) *The Psychiatric Interview*. New York: W.W. Norton.

Tageson, C.W. (1982) *Humanistic Psychology: A Synthesis*. Homewood, IL: Dorsey Press.

Tansey, M.H. and Burke, W.F. (1985) Projective identification and the empathic process: Interactional communications, *Contemporary Psychoanalysis*, 21: 42–69.

Thibaut, J. and Kelley, H.H. (1959) *The Social Psychology of Groups*. New York: Wiley.

Thorne, B.J. (1991) *Person-Centred Counselling: Therapeutic & Spiritual Dimensions*. London: Whurr.

Thorne, B.J. (1994) Developing a spiritual discipline, in D. Mearns (ed.) *Developing Person-Centred Counselling*. London: Sage.

Tobin, S.A. (1982) Self-disorders, Gestalt therapy and self-psychology, *The Gestalt Journal*, 5(2): 4–45.

Tournier, P. (1957) *The Meaning of Persons*. New York: Harper.

Treurniet, N. (1993) What is psychoanalysis now?, *International Journal of Psychoanalysis*, 74: 873–91.

Trop, J.L. and Stolorow, R.D. (1997) Therapeutic empathy: An intersubjective perspective, in A.C. Bohart and L.S. Greenberg (eds) *Empathy Reconsidered: New Directions in Psychotherapy*. Washington, DC: American Psychological Association.

Wachtel, P.L. (1986) On the limits of therapeutic neutrality, *Contemporary Psychoanalysis*, 22: 60–70.

Watson, J.B. and Reyner, R. (1920) Conditioned emotional reactions. *Journal of Experimental Psychology*, 3: 1–14.

Watson, J. C. and Greenberg, L.S. (1994) The alliance in experiential therapy: Enacting the relationship conditions, in A.O. Horvath and L.S. Greenberg (eds) *The Working Alliance: Theory, Research and Practice*. New York: Wiley.

Weigert, E. (1970) *The Courage to Love*. New Haven, CT: Yale University Press.

Weiner, J.P. and Boss, P. (1985) Exploring gender bias against women: Ethics for marriage and family therapy, *Counseling and Values*, 30: 9–23.

Weiss, J., Sampson, J. and the Mount Zion Psychotherapy Research Group (1986) *The Psychoanalytic Process: Theory, Clinical Observations and Empirical Research*. New York: Guilford Press.

Wheeler, G. (1995) Shame in two paradigms of therapy, *British Gestalt Journal*, 4(2).

Wilson, G.T. and Evans, I.M. (1977) The therapist–client relationship in behavior therapy, in A.S. Gurman and A.M. Razin (eds) *Effective Psychotherapy: A Handbook of Research*. New York: Pergamon Press.

Winer, R. (1994) *Close Encounters: A Relational View of the Therapeutic Process*. Northvale, NJ: Jason Aronson.

Winnicott, D.W. ([1947] 1992) Hate in the countertransference, in *Through Paediatrics to Psychoanalysis*. London: Karnac Books.

Winnicott, D.W. ([1954a] 1992) Metapsychological and clinical aspects of regression within the psycho-analytical set-up, in *Through Paediatrics to Psycho-Analysis*. London: Karnac Books.

Winnicott, D.W. ([1954b] 1992) The depressive position in normal emotional development, in *Through Paediatrics to Psycho-Analysis*. London: Karnac Books.

Winnicott, D.W. ([1956] 1992) Primary maternal preoccupation, in *Through Paediatrics to Psycho-Analysis*. London: Karnac Books.

Winnicott, D.W. ([1960a] 1990) The theory of the parent–infant relationship, in *The Maturational Processes and the Facilitating Environment*. London: Karnac Books.

Winnicott, D.W. ([1960b] 1990) Ego distortion in terms of true and false self, in *The Maturational Processes and the Facilitating Environment*. London: Karnac Books.

Winnicott, D.W. ([1963] 1990) Dependence in infant-care, in child-care, and in the psycho-analytic setting, in *The Maturational Processes and the Facilitating Environment*. London: Karnac Books.

Winnicott, D.W. ([1964] 1991) *The Child, the Family and the Outside World*. London: Penguin.

Winnicott, D.W. ([1965a] 1990) *The Maturational Processes and the Facilitating Environment*. London: Karnac Books.

Winnicott, D.W. ([1965b] 1989) *The Family and Individual Development*. London: Tavistock/Routledge.

Winnicott, D.W. ([1968] 1974) The use of an object and relating through identifications, in *Playing and Reality*. Harmondsworth: Penguin.

Winnicott, D.W. ([1971] 1974) *Playing and Reality*. Harmondsworth: Pelican.

Winnicott, D.W. (1974) Fear of breakdown, in C. Winnicott, R. Shepherd and M. Davis (eds) *Psycho-Analytic Explorations*. London: Karnac Books.

Wolf, E.S. (1983) Aspects of neutrality, *Psychoanalytic Inquiry*, 3: 675–89.

Wolf, E.S. (1991) Advances in self psychology: The evolution of psychoanalytic treatment, *Psychoanalytic Inquiry*, 2: 123–46.

Wolpe, J. (1954) Reciprocal inhibition as the main basis of psychotherapeutic effects, *American Medical Association Archives of Neurology and Psychiatry*, 72: 205–26.

Wolpe, J. (1958) *Psychotherapy by Reciprocal Inhibition*. Stanford, CA: Stanford University Press.

Wright, J.H. and Beck, A.T. (1994) Cognitive therapy, in R.E. Hales and S.C. Yudofsky (eds) *Synopsis of Psychiatry*. Washington, DC: American Psychiatric Press.

Yalom, I. (1980) *Existential Psychotherapy*. New York: Basic Books.

Yontef, G. ([1976] 1993) Gestalt therapy: Clinical phenomenology, in *Awareness, Dialogue and Process: Essays on Gestalt Therapy*. New York: Gestalt Journal Press.

Yontef, G. (1993) *Awareness, Dialogue and Process: Essays on Gestalt Therapy*. New York: Gestalt Journal Press.

Yontef, G. and Simkin, J. (1989) Gestalt therapy, in R. Corsini and D. Wedding (eds) *Current Psychotherapies*, 4th edn. Itasca, IL: Peacock.

Zetzel, E.R. ([1956] 1987) The concept of transference, in *The Capacity for Emotional Growth*. London: Karnac Books.

Zetzel, E.R. ([1958] 1987) Therapeutic alliance in the analysis of hysteria, in *The Capacity for Emotional Growth*. London: Karnac Books.

Zetzel, E.R. ([1970] 1987) *The Capacity for Emotional Growth*. London: Karnac Books.

Index